WEBELOS
3

MY NAME IS:

Roman Fail

**I EARNED MY
BOBCAT BADGE:** Mar. 31, 1979

**I BELONG TO
WEBELOS DEN:** Den I #1

PACK: 338

DATE: 5-29-81

Phone: 466-5840

Add.: 7441 Daytona
LemonGrove, Ca
92045

WEBELOS

SCOUT BOOK

Library of Congress Catalog Card Number 67-14536   No. 3232   300M980   ISBN 0-8395-3232-6

CONTENTS

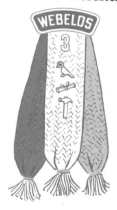

IF YOU ARE JUST STARTING
WE ARE GLAD YOU JOINED!

WELCOME

TO THE WEBELOS DEN

If you are 10 years old or have completed the fourth grade and just joining the pack, the first thing you do is register, then pass the Bobcat requirements.

Get an application to join a pack. Fill it out, have your parents sign it, and give it to your Webelos leader together with the registration fee. Then go to work on your Bobcat requirements, explained on pages 279-83. As you complete them, have your parents sign your book.

1. Learn and give the Cub Scout Promise.

2. Say the Law of the Pack. Tell what it means.

3. Tell what Webelos means.

4. Show the Cub Scout sign and handshake. Tell what they mean.

5. Give Cub Scout motto and salute. Tell what they mean.

Bobcat completed   parent ok   date

WEBELOS

·WE-BE-LO-S

WE'LL BE LOYAL SCOUTS

WELCOME TO THE WEBELOS DEN!

You are now a Webelos Scout and a member of the older boys' den. You must be 10 years old or have completed the fourth grade to join this den.

Do your best today to be prepared for tomorrow.

Everyone knows that Webelos Scouts are the oldest boys in the pack. Because they are, they often can throw a ball farther than most Cub Scouts. They can hit a ball harder, too.

Webelos Scouts are always on the trail of something new. Webelos Scouts are curious, interested, enthusiastic, and active.

3

WEBELOS

WEBELOS: Say Wee'-buh-lows.

Webelos has a secret meaning for Cub Scouts. It means:

WE'll BE LOyal Scouts.

Loyal means that you will keep your Cub Scout promise.

Webelos Scouts wear the Webelos badge colors and den number on their right sleeve. You get your badge colors when you become a member of a den. Your Cubmaster or Webelos den leader will give you your colors.

Ask your mother to take off your old den number. Pin on your Webelos badge colors. Look on the inside of the back cover of this book for directions.

IF YOU HAVE NEVER BEEN A CUB SCOUT BE-FORE: You will learn the Cub Scout Promise when you become a Webelos den member. You will be taught the Law of the Pack. You can find them on page 280 of this book. Other Cub Scouting signs and secrets are there too.

THE WEBELOS DEN MEETING

Your Webelos den will meet early on one evening or on Saturday each week. Here you may work on the requirements for activity badges that you want.

You will learn new skills and improve your work in the things you already know. Go to all the meetings and get plenty of practice.

Sometimes the Webelos den will go on special outings. All of this is meant to prepare you to become a Scout.

THE PACK MEETING

The Webelos den plays a big part in pack meetings. The Cubmaster may ask you to help set up the room. You may guide parents to their seats. You may be asked to show some of the skills that you have learned. These would be things that the younger boys could not do.

At each pack meeting, there is a special ceremony. This is for the Webelos Scouts who have earned badges during the month. You will get your badge from your Webelos den leader at this meeting.

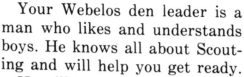

Your Webelos den leader is a man who likes and understands boys. He knows all about Scouting and will help you get ready.

He will teach you the right way to do many things that are fun. Things like building a fire and cooking a meal. He will be a good guide on the road to Scouting.

Your den leader knows the importance of "Do Your Best." He will help you to improve your skills and to learn new ones.

He knows the importance of ideals. He believes in God and the greatness of America. He believes in you and the man that you will become one day. This is why he takes the time to lead your Webelos den.

Attending all den meetings and other activities is a way to say thanks to your leader.

ASK YOUR FRIENDS TO JOIN

Other boys you know may want to become Webelos. Tell them about it. Take them to a den meeting. If they are 10 years old or have completed the fourth grade, they can join.

IF THEY HAVE NEVER BEEN CUB SCOUTS

You earned Bobcat long ago. Now the Webelos den leader will ask them to do this too. Show them what they will have to do. It is on page 278 of this book.

WEBELOS DEN CHIEF

Your Webelos den chief will be a Scout or Explorer. He will know how to lead Webelos Scouts. Probably, he will be older than the den chief that you had as a Cub Scout.

WEBELOS DENNER

A den member will be elected as the Webelos denner to help the den chief. You might be the one to be chosen.

YOUR NEW UNIFORM

As the Indian boy became older, he became wiser in his people's ways. He changed his boy's clothes for those of a warrior. So you will change your uniform, adding the parts of a Webelos Scout.

7

You can earn money for your uniform. Here are some ways. Make and sell handicraft articles. Weed gardens. Shovel snow. Mow lawns. Clean windows. Wash cars or dogs. Care for pets while their owners are away. Baby-sit. Run errands.

The new parts of your uniform tell everyone that you are an older Cub Scout. People know that you belong to the Webelos den. They know that you expect to become a Scout when you leave the pack. Wear your uniform on all Scouting activities. Wear it hiking and for service projects and shows. Wear it for Scouting's anniversary month activities and den and pack meetings.

YOUR NECKERCHIEF

You may wear a neckerchief with V-necked or regular shirts. Turn collar of regular shirt under to wear neckerchief.

Here's how to wear it:

Roll long edge over and over several times to about 6 inches from the tip.

Place rolled neckerchief around your neck. Pull neckerchief slide up snugly. Tie or keep ends loose according to the rule of your pack.

Neckerchief should fit smoothly on back of shirt, 6 inches from tip to top of fold.

ACTIVITY BADGES

These are the activity badges you can earn. They should help to satisfy your 10-year-old curiosity. You can earn all 15 of them or as many as you want. It depends upon how much "get up and go" you have.

AQUANAUT

NATURALIST

CITIZEN

GEOLOGIST

FORESTER

SCHOLAR

SCIENTIST

TRAVELER

SHOWMAN

OUTDOORSMAN

ARTIST

CRAFTSMAN

ENGINEER

ATHLETE

SPORTSMAN

Just think of it! In earning the Aquanaut badge, you will learn to swim 100 feet. Of that distance, 50 feet will be on your back. You might also learn to swim on the surface with mask, snorkel, and fins. You will look at the wonders of the underwater world. You may also learn how to handle a rowboat, to surface dive, and to rescue someone.

As a forester, you'll learn about trees and the animals that use them. You'll find out how to plant and care for small trees and how to prevent forest fires.

The geologist studies volcanoes, geysers, earthquakes, and rocks. As an outdoorsman, you will learn how to live comfortably in the outdoors. On the dad-and-son overnights, you can try out what you have learned.

Backyard camping, family camping, and fun around a campfire are big helps to you. How? They prepare you for the Scout camping adventures, less than a year away.

Whole new worlds open as you dig into the Naturalist badge. Your own zoo, studying wild animals, and keeping an aquarium are all part of it.

What makes things happen? That is the big question to a scientist. The Scientist badge, then, is for the curious. Do you want to add to what you know and can learn to do? Learn about air and water, balancing tricks, and optical illusions as part of this badge.

Engineer, Artist, Craftsman, Sportsman, Scholar, Athlete, Citizen, Showman, Traveler—which of these do you like? They can start you down the trail to Scouting. You can feel at home when you start on Scout merit badges.

Your den leader or some other interested person will work with you. He will help you to understand and

to handle the harder things in the activity badges.

Your Webelos den program usually will use an activity badge subject. Each week you will work on one or more of the requirements for that badge. You will be given credit for each skill as you do it. You may be very interested in one activity badge. If you are, you can do all of the requirements and earn the badge.

You may work at any time on any activity badge area that you want. You don't have to wait for a den meeting. Practice skills with another den member or with your dad. Go to your den leader when you think that you can pass the tests. He will pass you or will ask someone else to help you. (This might be another dad or the den chief.) He will check and pass you if you do the tests well.

What are the real values to be gained from your badge work? You become good at new skills. You learn to make things go and understand why. The badge tells the world that you can stick to something. It means a job, a game or an exercise has been done and done well.

The activity badges are just for Webelos Scouts.

Many of the things you do in den meetings will count as work toward activity badges. In one of your den meetings, you might take part in an outdoor campfire. This could count toward your Outdoorsman badge.

On a den or pack picnic, you might run a 50-yard dash. You might do a standing long jump. If you do either well enough, it would count toward your Athlete badge.

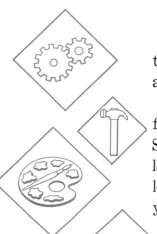

For Wolf and Bear, you passed tests to your parents. They signed for your achievements and electives.

Do you think that you can pass things for an activity badge? As a Webelos Scout, you will go to your Webelos den leader. He will pass you or ask another leader to watch your work and pass you.

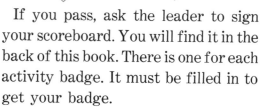

If you pass, ask the leader to sign your scoreboard. You will find it in the back of this book. There is one for each activity badge. It must be filled in to get your badge.

You will get the badge in a ceremony at a pack meeting. It will be a metal badge to be worn on your badge colors.

The activity badge colors are worn on the right arm. The metal activity badges, as earned, are fastened to any one of the colors. Don't wear more than five badges on any one color.

THE WEBELOS BADGE

When you have earned three activity badges, you will have completed the first requirement for the Webelos badge. The fourth rank in Cub Scout advancement, it includes learning about Boy Scout requirements, the meaning of the Scout badge, the Outdoor Code, and your uniform. Next step, the Arrow of Light Award.

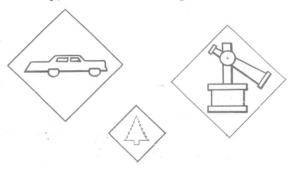

THE ARROW OF LIGHT AWARD

This is Cub Scouting's highest rank and most prized award. You may start to earn it when you have joined a Webelos den and have earned your Webelos badge. The Webelos badge and Arrow of Light will prepare you to help others appreciate the outdoors and understand more about the Scout program.

AQUANAUT

An aquanaut is a person who is at home in and around the water. He respects the water, he masters it, and he enjoys it.

The aquanaut knows that water can be dangerous. He never takes foolish chances or breaks safety rules. He knows that rules protect him as well as others.

He builds up his water skills. Then he knows that he is safe in and on the water. The better he becomes, the more fun he has.

ARE YOU AN AQUANAUT?

The tests in this activity area will tell you. You will enjoy trying them. If you can't quite do all of them now, keep trying them. You will be improving all the time. These tests will help you to get ready for more advanced aquatics in Scouting.

DO: Swim 100 feet, half of this with the elementary backstroke.

AND DO THREE:

Do a surface dive and swim underwater for at least two strokes before coming up.

Swim on the surface for 50 feet properly using a mask, fins, and snorkel.

Know the rules of small-boat safety. Show that you know how to handle a rowboat.

Explain three of the four basic rescue methods.

HAVE FUN—BE SAFE

Swimming and boating are lots of fun. They can lead to even greater adventure when you grow up.

Know the dangers around water. Work on your swimming and boating skills. You'll be safer if you do. Knowing how, safe gear, and knowing what to do are important. They will make sure you have a great time and come back safely.

For your own safety, know how far you can swim. Swim in water safe for you. Stay in water not over 3½ feet deep if you can't swim. If you can swim 50 feet, you may go in water 6 feet deep. If you can swim 100 yards or more, you may swim in water over 6 feet deep. Make plans to improve your swimming and then do it. Practice kicks and strokes until strong and sure.

ALWAYS SWIM WITH A BUDDY

This is good safety common sense for all ages. You and your buddy can help each other if either of you gets into trouble. You can help each other to improve by making a game of practicing. The buddy plan is used in all swimming in Scouting.

Rules on the waterfront are to protect you. Cross out a Do or Don't on each line to make the rules read correctly:

DO DON'T show off in the water.

DO DON'T dive into strange waters.

DO DON'T go in swimming right after eating.

DO DON'T have your family physician tell you of any problems found in your fitness checkup. You can then swim with confidence.

AQUANAUTS SWIM WELL

Any would-be aquanaut needs to learn to swim well. Each different stroke has its value. It can be learned easily with the help of a swimming coach or teacher. Follow the pictures and directions for doing the elementary backstroke, sidestroke, and crawl—the right way.

ELEMENTARY BACKSTROKE

Start by floating on your back, arms down at your sides.

Bring your cupped hands up over your chest to your shoulders. Then reach straight outward. Sweep your arms down to your sides.

At the same time that you start the arm movement, drop your heels downward. They should be beneath your knees. Turn your toes outward. Without stopping, swing your feet outward in a circular motion. They should come together in a straight-out position, with toes pointed. The arm pull and leg kick happen at the same time. You should end up the same way you were at the start.

Keep your eyes looking down toward your feet over the surface of the water.

SIDESTROKE

Lie on your side with one ear in the water. Stretch your under arm out ahead of you. Your top arm will be along your leg.

Start with your feet together and move your heels toward your hips.

Cup your reaching hand a little. Sweep it down in front of your chest.

Move your feet apart. Move your top leg forward and your bottom leg backward.

Notice the hand and arm movement. As one hand pushes down, the other is brought up. They meet.

When your legs are as far apart as possible, snap them together like closing a pair of scissors.

The upper hand is pushing down. Your lower hand is going back to where it was at the start.

Stop your feet as they come together. Repeat arm and leg movements.

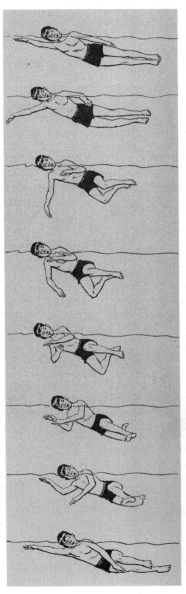

THE CRAWL STROKE

Float facedown in the water with arms and legs extended.

Move legs up and down. Press down on the water with the top of your foot.

Still kicking, pull downward with your right arm. Breathe out through your nose while your face is in the water.

As right-arm stroke ends, begin stroke with left. Raise your face by turning your head to the right so you can breathe in through your mouth.

Reach ahead again with your right arm.

At the end of the left-arm stroke, begin a new one with the right arm. Turn your face underwater again to breathe out.

Keep even strokes and leg kicks.

The crawl stroke is a fast way to swim, but it is tiring. It is great for races and swimming for a short way.

AQUANAUTS KNOW WATER RESCUE METHODS

Boys are not expected to do the rescue work of a trained adult. Still, they should know some simple rescues. These might save a person in trouble when no one else was around.

The order of methods to choose is

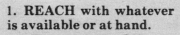

1. REACH with whatever is available or at hand.

2. THROW a line, a buoy, a floating object to provide support.

3. ROW a boat, canoe, or raft—anything to help hold up the victim safely.

4. GO Swimming rescues are for trained older people. They are dangerous for the rescuer unless he knows what to do.

These rescues are taught as a part of the Scout Lifesaving merit badge.

SURFACE DIVE

Float facedown with arms out ahead of you. Sweep the arms back toward your hips.

At the same time, bend forward sharply at the hips. Aim the top part of your body toward the bottom.

Turn hands palm down. Push them toward the bottom. Raise your legs above the surface as high as you can.

Your head will be pointing downward. The weight of your legs in the air above the water will drive you down.

Swim underwater for two strokes before coming to the top again.

SNORKELING

Would you like to become a real "snorkler"? Learn to use face mask, swim fins, and snorkel. First you must be a good swimmer. You must be able to surface dive and to swim underwater.

Your vision is blurred underwater by the water against your eyes. A face mask puts air in front of your eyes. This helps you to see clearly. Let's see what makes a good mask. It should cover only the eyes and nose. If you held it to your face and breathed in, what should happen? It should fit so well that it clings to your face without the head strap. The window should be of safety glass. It should have a metal band to hold the glass tightly in place. Adding a snorkel should not break the seal between your face and the mask.

When you go underwater with a face mask, it may fog over. To stop

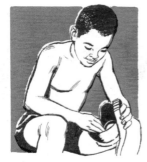

this, treat it first. Spit on the glass. Rub it around. Then rinse the glass. Fogging will be cut down a lot.

Try out your face mask in shallow water. There you will have a clear view of the things that are in the water. Interesting things of water nature lore are waiting for you to find around a pond or lake shore. Only the time that you can hold your breath limits your view. When you need to breathe, raise your head from the water and breathe through your mouth. This is the only way to breathe when using a face mask.

You can move about the surface with face underwater, see things beneath, and still breathe. How? You can use a snorkel. This is a J-shaped tube with a soft rubber end to fit in your mouth. It has an open tube reaching up through which you can breathe.

When you use a snorkel, put it inside the headband of your mask. It should slope backward. The mouth-piece should be held in your mouth. Blow out before you breathe through your snorkel. Breathe only at the surface. Feel the back of your head to see if the tube is out of the water. If it is, then you can breathe through it.

You can go faster on the surface by using swim fins. There are several kinds. Some have heel straps and others have full foot pockets. The ones with heel straps fit any foot, because the size of the straps can be changed. The ones with pockets must be fitted to your feet. They can't be too tight nor too loose. They give protection like shoes when walking on rough or sharp rocks. They cost more than the strap kind.

Fins give your feet more surface area in the water. This is like the way a fish's tail or fins work. Use slow, easy flutter kicks. Keep your knees well bent. This will move you through the water at a good speed. Don't work too hard at first. Your legs will tire quickly. Train slowly. Build your ability until you can use them for a longer time.

When you swim, your body is at

the surface. Looking through your mask and breathing through your snorkel, your eyes and thoughts are below. Unless you are a good swimmer, don't dive under until you are older. When you get good at skindiving, you can dive down. Then you can see many wonderful underwater sights right in front of your eyes.

Wise aquanauts obey the chief point of all aquatic safety and

NEVER SWIM ALONE!
ALWAYS USE THE BUDDY SYSTEM.

While snorkeling, stay near your buddy at all times.

Never overbreathe (called hyperventilation) before trying to swim underwater. Take regular breaths. When you feel you want to breathe, do so right away by lifting your face. Then you won't be taking a chance on underwater blackout.

AQUANAUTS ARE SAFE BOATMEN

Aquanauts may use a rowboat, a motorboat, or any other type of watercraft. They keep in mind the safe ways of handling a boat.

The rules and drawings show the right ways. The rest is up to you.

BOAT SAFETY

Know your boat—don't overload it. In a rowboat, one person per seat is a pretty safe rule. Have life jackets in the boat, one for each person. Non-swimmers wear theirs.

Balance your load. Divide weight evenly from side to side and bow to stern.

Step into your boat. Step in center when boarding or changing seats and always keep low.

If your boat tips over or fills up with water, hang on. You can kick the boat to shore or drift in, but don't leave it. Let help come to you.

Watch the weather. Head for shore when it looks bad. If you are caught out, seat your passengers on the floor. Head your boat into the waves.

If you use a motor, use the right one. Too much power can damage your boat or even swamp it. Look on the back of the boat for the OBC (Outboard Boating Club of America) plate. It shows how many people the boat should hold and the recommended horsepower. Don't make sharp turns—they are dangerous. Take it easy.

Keep a sharp lookout for other boats and swimmers.

AQUANAUT
SCOREBOARD

Requirements

ARTIST

You have worked with the tools of art all your life. You have used paints, crayons, pencils, and clay. At home and school you have made pictures and shapes.

In this activity area you can learn more about how artists work. You will learn how they mix colors, make designs, and make mobiles and sculptures.

You may not have a talent for art. But even if you don't, you will have fun learning how artists do it.

COMPLETE FIVE OF THE FOLLOWING:

- Draw or paint an original picture. Use watercolor, crayons, or oil. Frame it for your room or home.
- List the primary and secondary colors. Tell how to combine colors.
- Make six designs using straight lines, curved lines, or both.
- Make a profile of a member of your family.
- Use plastic or clay and sculpture a simple object.
- Make a mobile.
- Make a construction. Use your own choice of materials. Examples are dowels, screen wire, cellophane, and string.

OIL PAINTING

● Equipment ● Work place ● Layout

Still lifes and landscapes are the best subjects for the beginner painting with oils. Red, yellow, and blue are the primary colors. See what you can do with them. Then try white with them. Paint several small squares using different color combinations. Add white to lighten or black to darken. Practice over and over with brush and palette knife.

Begin by painting a vase, a box, or a bottle. Try fruit—a banana, an apple, an orange, or a pear. Paint it several times. The more you practice, the better your picture.

Copy a still-life picture that you like. Try to capture the highlights, the shadows, the freshness of the picture you are copying.

Now set up your own still-life picture. Use different shaped objects, fruits, or vegetables—some round, some tall, some long, some short. Try for a pleasant arrangement of a few things.

In making up landscapes, avoid cutting the picture in half, up and down, or across. The horizon should be just above or below the picture's center. A road, a path, or an opening in the trees should call to the viewer. He should feel that he could go into the picture. Use a bend in the road or a good balance to do this.

USING THE BRUSH

Draw in your subjects lightly with pencil or brush, then start painting.

Hold your brush as you would a pencil or a candle—whichever suits you better. Either way, hold it well back from the brush end.

Practice will make the brush become a part of your hand. You'll forget all about how to hold it. You'll reach out and put color right where you want it.

A PLACE OF YOUR OWN

A painter needs a place to call his own. He should have a spot where he can leave an unfinished canvas on an easel. His paints and brushes should be safe there.

Go slow in buying your equipment at first. Check with the art teacher at school or an artist friend. Get a good beginners' book from the library. Look at some books in an art store.

Buy the best things that you can and take good care of them. Cap your paint tubes after each use. This keeps the paint from drying out. Clean your brushes well. Then you'll get true color the next time you use them.

OIL PAINTS IN TUBES

Buy studio-size tubes in artist grade for best results.

Alizarin crimson
Cadmium red, light
Cadmium yellow, light
Yellow ochre
Burnt sienna
Raw umber
Viridian green
Ultramarine blue
Titanium white
Black
Turpentine—rectified
Linseed oil—purified
Damar varnish
Charcoal—medium
Kneaded eraser • Pencil
Fixative and sprayer • Gum eraser

YOUR PAINTBOX

A cardboard carton or shoebox should do. It should be large enough to hold your things. These would be palette, canvas board, paints, oilcup, rags, knives, and brushes.

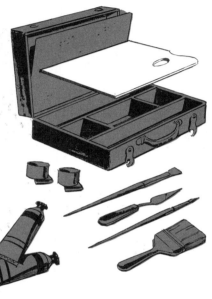

BRUSHES

Bristle—flats No. 2—No. 8;
    brights No. 2—No. 12
Sable No. 6
House painter's brush—
    No. 2 flat
Palette knife
Painting knife

Rags
Canvas boards
Palette
Oilcup (double—metal)

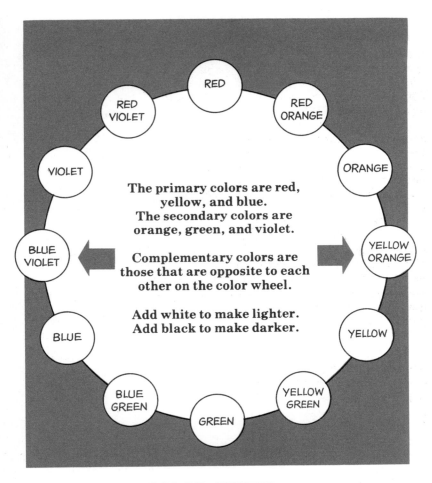

The primary colors are red, yellow, and blue.
The secondary colors are orange, green, and violet.

Complementary colors are those that are opposite to each other on the color wheel.

Add white to make lighter.
Add black to make darker.

COLOR WHEEL

Follow the color wheel in mixing color. Mix a little blue with yellow to make green. The more blue, the darker the green. Mix red with yellow to get orange. The more red, the deeper the orange. Mix blue with red to get violet. The more blue, the deeper the color.

Mix small amounts with your brush and watch the colors come to life. This is the real fun. Practice, practice, and practice, mixing colors. Remember what happens in each mix.

DESIGN

Design is the arrangement of lines or shapes in ways that are eye pleasing.

Nature is full of designs. Think of the shapes of flowers and the way leaves are on a stem. Think of frost on window glass and the beauty of snowflakes. Color adds to a design's beauty. Notice the "eyes" on a butterfly wing, the bars and spots on a flying bird. Look at the color on bees and wasps and the faces on flowers.

How should you start on a design? You might just begin drawing. Use a piece of paper, a ruler, and a pencil, crayon, or paintbrush. Simply doodle until you see something that you like. Try to keep your design simple and give it balance. When you finish, it should look just right. It should have no extra lines and no lines missing.

You say you don't have any ideas for a design? All right, try this.

Take your young brother's set of Tinker Toys. If he doesn't have any, use some crayons and pencils.

Drop the whole mess on the floor. Now you've got something that looks like this:

Not very pleasing to the eye, is it? Try moving the Tinker Toys around. If you have an orderly mind, you might come up with something like this:

Is your sport baseball? Use homeplate, the pitcher's mound, and first, second, and third base to make a design.

Try nature. A tree or a bush might give you an idea. Here's a tree design:

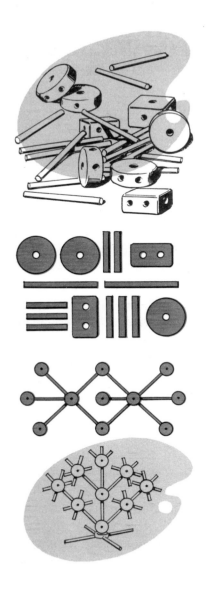

These are all good designs. Copy them in a balanced arrangement and you'll have a pleasing design.

Designers work with more than just straight and curved lines. If you want to add variety to your design, try using simple figures like this.

Or you might use shapes like these.

Designs are all around us. The wallpaper in your home is one. A magazine cover is, too, even if it's only a picture and the magazine's name.

Look them over with an eye for their design. They may give you ideas for some designs of your own. Don't copy them. The fun is in dreaming up your own ideas.

When you have drawn a design, you may want to add color. Do that with paint or crayons. Remember, you want your design to be balanced. Use color to do this just as you used lines.

Maybe you will want to decorate something with one of your designs. You can put it on wood by using cutout figures, painting, or simple carving. Perhaps you wish to put a design on leather. See page 240 of this book for help.

MOBILES-DESIGNS IN DEPTH

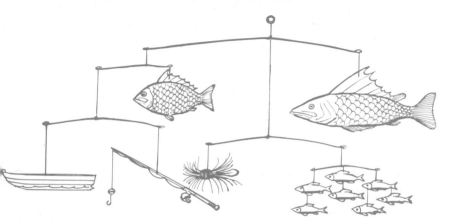

Mobiles can be interesting decorations for many rooms in the house. Make them by putting pieces together in a balanced design. They move in the slightest breeze.

A display of your father's hobbies would make a nice mobile for his den. In the kitchen, how about a "menu mobile"? You could use pictures of meats, vegetables, and drinks.

Make the designs from wire, cardboard, foil, thin wood, or metal. Find the balance point of each piece. Do this by putting a pin near the top edge of the design. When you find the balance point, punch or drill two holes right below it. Use this to fasten your design to the arms of the mobile. Then it balances.

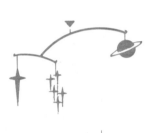

- You should make a mobile from the bottom up. It will be easier. You won't have to make so many changes as you go along.
- Coat-hanger wire is good for the arms. Cut a length each of 12 inches, 19 inches, 24 inches, and 25 inches.
- Straighten each wire arm by hammering or pressing in a vice. Then bend it into a smooth arc.
- Bend up each piece about ½ inch from the ends. Make right angles to the curve.
- Hang a design on each end of one wire arm. Flatten the ends of the wire to hold the thread in place.
- Tie a thread on the wire arm and slide it until the two designs balance. Make a loop with the thread here on top of the arc. With spool wire, make a small ring through this loop.
- Fasten another design to one end of the second wire and flatten that end. Place the other end in the ring on the first wire. Flatten that end to hold the first wire in place.
- Find the balance point of the mobile as you did for the first arm. Again make a thread loop above the second arm's arc at the balance point. Add a ring made of spool wire.
- Add the other wire arm and designs in the same way. Hang the mobile from kite string, fishing line, or strong thread.

Dowels may be used in place of wire. If you use them, hang the designs with thread, ribbon, or string. Find balance point on rod and tie length of string at this point.

CONSTRUCTIONS

Constructions are fun. They are simple designs in space. Start with a handful of clay or a box for a base. Or use a piece of wood or heavy cardboard. Even a Tinker Toy set or a piece of pipe will do. Add things to it or remove things from it until your design pleases you.

Collect odds and ends—wooden or plastic spoons, forks, and knives; tongue depressors; lace; and ribbon. Save ice cream sticks, bits of wood, buttons, flashbulbs, wire, seashells, string, cloth, and yarn. Find chicken wire, pipe cleaners, screen wire, spools, corks, pine cones, nuts, and small boxes. Seed pods, feathers, toothpicks, straws, keys, bottle caps, and costume jewelry are good. So are odd earrings, Christmas ornaments, and pieces of colored plastic.

Start with your base. You can push the main wire or stick right into clay. If using wood, you may have to drill or punch holes.

WOOD BASE

- Drill holes for wire. Put in ends. Bend out to hold in place.
- Drill holes for sticks. Put in. Tie together at the top.
- Crisscross with yarn, wire, or string.
- Add decorations until the design pleases you.

CARDBOARD BASE

Punch two holes for each wire in your cardboard base. Put in the wires down and up through the holes. Bend the wires any way you like. Form a column, circle, square, diamond, or rectangle. Add things from your collection.

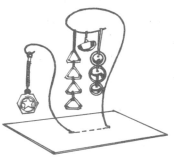

Try twisting pieces of screen wire, hardware cloth, or chicken wire into different shapes. Use them as a base. Or lift them into the air on lengths of wire, dowel, or plastic material. Use the screen for your design's background.

SCULPTURE

When you have a piece of clay in your hands, what happens? You squeeze it, twist it, pull it, roll it, and shape it with your thumbs. You push in two spots for eyes with your fingers. You add small bits of clay, building up the nose, the chin, and the neck. Ears and hair come next. You take a pinch off here. You add a little more there. You turn your work around. You look at it closely from the top, the sides, the back, and the front. You even check under the chin.

Your best tools for working clay are your fingers. Sometimes, however, you will want or need a tool. Just whittle one in the shape you need. You can find pictures of them at the library. Or your art teacher at school will let you see them.

WHAT TO WORK WITH

Plasteline, a commercial modeling clay, is oily and plastic. It never dries out. It works easily when kept at room temperature.

If something stops your work, put it away until you can return to it. You'll find that it is still soft and ready to be worked. Plasteline costs a little more than clay in the beginning. But, you'll save money in the long run. It can be used over and over again.

MOIST CLAY

Clay can be found in many places. It comes from the earth. It can be worked easily when damp. As it dries, it becomes stiffer and is good for detail work. Because natural clay does dry out, it must be kept covered when not being worked. Use wet cloths and a plastic bag. If it dries out you can reclaim it. Soak it and knead it until it becomes soft again.

SELF-HARDENING CLAY

This is a prepared clay. It costs more than the moist kind. It is as easily worked, as long as it is kept wet and soft. It is self-drying and becomes very hard. When it has dried, it cannot be softened for reuse.

When you start, make your heads small, about 3 or 4 inches wide. This size needs less clay. Yet it is still large enough for you to work on detail. If you have a head that you like, make a plaster cast of it. Then cast some puppet heads.

Work in a well-lighted room. Your workbench or table should be solid. The clay should be at eye level. Do this by sitting on a chair or stool lower than your work. Or put your clay on a box on top of it.

Work in a place that is easy to clean. Clay dropped on a good floor or rug leaves stains.

47

1. Make a support. Use a piece of broomstick or 1-inch dowel 12 inches long. Drill a 1-inch hole in the center of a 6- by 6-inch block of wood.

2. Mount the clay on and around the dowel stick. Build up an egg shape about 3½ inches wide.

3. Then push in the eyes with your thumbs.

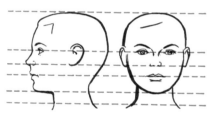

4. Note the shape of the normal head. Most beginners forget the forehead and back of the head.

5. Add clay to build up the chin, nose, neck, brows, and ears.

6. Refine lips, eyes, and shape of the head.

ARTIST
SCOREBOARD

Requirements

ATHLETE

Strength and good health are important to you now for sports and games. They will be important to you all of your life. This is so, even when you reach your grandfather's age and are not so active.

You are older now. Soon you will be starting in Scouting. You should be strong enough to take the rough, outdoor life of a Scout.

Now is the time to see how you measure up to some standards. The tests for strength and endurance will tell how you rate.

You will find a scoring table for each of the exercises. It will show how you are doing. Try to meet the top rating. Maybe you won't be able to the first time you try. Don't let that stop you. The more you work at each exercise, the higher your rating should be.

When you become a Scout, you will promise to keep yourself physically strong. Prepare for this now.

COMPLETE FOUR OF THE FOLLOWING PROJECTS:

- Lie on your back. Hook your feet under something heavy to hold them down. Do 30 sit-ups.

- Do two pull-ups on a bar or eight push-ups from the ground or floor.

- Do a standing long jump of at least 5 feet.

- Do a 50-yard dash in 8.6 seconds or less.

- Jump into water over your head. Level off and swim 50 feet. Turn over on your back and rest in a floating position for 15 seconds. Then swim back to the starting point. Have a grown-up who swims well watching.

- Do a 600-yard run (walk) in 2 minutes 45 seconds or less.

The Boy Scouts of America has a set of physical tests. Their purpose is to determine muscular strength and endurance. There are standards for boys from 10 to 17 years old.

The five tests on the following pages will show how well you can do. Have your Webelos den leader test you. Then put the scores on your Fitness Progress Chart, page 55.

These same exercises will be used to test you as you get older. Each set of results should be written on your chart.

SIT-UPS

STARTING POSITION: Lie on your back with legs out, feet about a foot apart. Put hands behind neck with fingers interlaced. Have a partner hold your ankles to keep your heels on the floor. He should count each sit-up.

ACTION: Sit up. Turn body to the left. Touch right elbow to left knee. Return to starting position. Sit up and turn body to the right. Touch left elbow to right knee. Return to the starting position.

One sit-up is counted each time you go back to the starting position.

NUMBER OF SIT-UPS		
Age	10	11
Excellent	60	67
Good	47	50
Satisfactory.....	30	31
Poor	22	23

PULL-UPS

EQUIPMENT: Use a bar high enough and easy to grip.

STARTING POSITION: Hold the bar with your thumbs facing one another. Hang with your arms and legs fully out, feet not touching the floor.

ACTION: Pull body up with arms until chin is over the bar. Then lower body until arms are straight.

RULES: The pull must not be a snap movement. Knees must not be raised or legs kicked. The body must not swing. If this happens, your partner should stop the motion. One pull-up is counted each time you place your chin over the bar.

NUMBER OF PULL-UPS		
Age	10	11
Excellent	6	6
Good	3	4
Satisfactory.....	2	2
Poor	1	1

STANDING LONG JUMP

EQUIPMENT: You will need a level surface and tape measure.

STARTING POSITION: Stand with your feet apart and your toes just behind the starting line. Prepare to jump by bending your knees and swinging your arms back and forth.

ACTION: Jump, swinging your arms ahead and upward hard. Take off from the balls of your feet.

RULES: Three trials are allowed. Distance is measured from the starting line. It runs to the place nearest the starting line that your body touches. Record the best of the three jumps.

DISTANCE JUMPED				
Age	10		11	
	ft.	in.	ft.	in.
Excellent ...	5	6	5	10
Good	5	0	5	4
Satisfactory.	4	8	5	0
Poor	4	4	4	7

50-YARD DASH

STARTING POSITION: Stand behind the starting line. The starter will be at the finish. He will have a stopwatch. He will raise one hand before giving the starting signal.

ACTION: The starter lowers his hand and hits the side of his leg. This is the signal to start. As you cross the finish line, the time is noted.

RULES: The score is the time between the starter's signal and the instant you cross the finish line.

IN SECONDS TO THE NEAREST TENTH		
Age	10	11
Excellent	7.6	7.3
Good	8.1	7.9
Satisfactory.....	8.6	8.3
Poor	9.0	8.7

600-YARD RUN (WALK)

STARTING POSITION: Stand behind the starting line. **ACTION:** On the signal "Ready—Go!" begin running. **RULES:** You can run or walk. However, you want to cover the distance in the shortest possible time. Record time in minutes and seconds.

IN MINUTES AND SECONDS		
Age	10	11
Excellent	2:15	2:12
Good	2:30	2:24
Satisfactory.....	2:45	2:37
Poor	2:58	2:50

Don't try to set a record the first time out. Practice each day. Slowly build up your pace. Remember, you can walk.

A football field can be used for the running tests. The 50-yard dash would be half the field between goal lines. The 600-yard run (walk) would be six lengths of the field.

INDIVIDUAL FITNESS RECORDS

FITNESS PROGRESS CHART

Name _____

Pack _____ Medical Checkup _____
(Date)

TEST	No. 1	No. 2	No. 3	No. 4	No. 5
DATE					
Pull-Ups					
Sit-Ups					
50-Yard Dash					
600-Yard Run (Walk)					
Standing Long Jump					

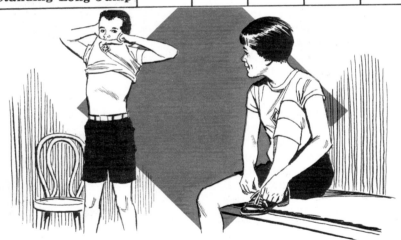

Exercises, contests, games, and activities are on the next page. Use them to help improve. Then you'll be able to meet the standards for your age.

INDIVIDUAL EXERCISES FOR
WEBELOS SCOUTS

Webelos Scouts should spend at least 15 minutes a day in exercises. You should do these by yourself, not with a group. Exercises help build muscles.

The ones shown on these pages need little or no equipment. They are the kind that you can do in or around your home. Active games, sports, swimming, hobbies calling for action, and home chores will strengthen you, too.

PAPER CRUNCH: This will build strong hands and fingers. Squeezing sticks, rocks, or sponge balls, hand wrestling, and rowing boats will also develop hands.

BICEP BUILDER: Push up with the left hand and arm. Push down with the right hand at the same time. Hold as you count to 10. Repeat five times for each arm.

TRUNK STRETCH: Strengthens the back and stretches the chest muscles. Lie facedown with hands at back of neck and elbows out. Raise head and chest and hold.

BRIDGE: Builds the neck and shoulders. Lie on back with feet flat. Push head down and raise buttocks and shoulders. Return to starting position and repeat.

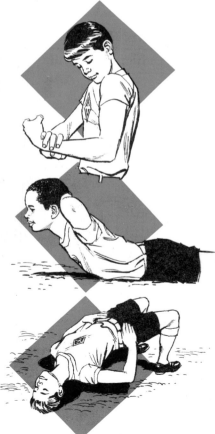

56

STRETCHER: Done best in slow motion. Curl up body slowly from flat-on-back position until the knees touch chin. Count five. Return to starting position.

ALL THE WAY: Strengthens stomach muscles for tough jobs. Lie with back on floor, hands above head. With arms and legs straight, raise body and touch toes.

NECK BUILDER: You need a good bath towel. Pull it hard across the back of your neck. Hold until neck muscles shake. Use hands in place of towel.

PUSH-UPS: Arm and shoulder builder. Keep back and legs straight while lowering and raising body. Build strong muscles by doing 20 push-ups daily.

HORIZONTAL BAR: Helps build arms and shoulders. Use hands to move across bar, ladder, or pipe. Practice on a pipe hung securely in basement or garage.

57

BUTTERFLY: Strengthens the back. Lie on stomach. Raise arms, chest, and legs. Spread arms and legs 10 times. Return to starting position and repeat.

TRUNK BEND: Strengthens trunk muscles. Bend sideways and down. Touch toes—first left, then right. Spread legs. Keep elbows and knees straight.

LEG STRETCH: Builds stomach muscles. Raise and spread legs slowly three times without touching floor. Hold 10 seconds, lower legs, and rest. Repeat.

SQUAT THRUST: Assume squat position, hands in front on floor. Thrust legs back until body is straight from shoulders to feet. Return to squat. Stand up.

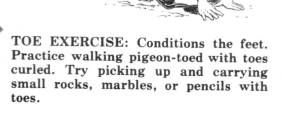

TOE EXERCISE: Conditions the feet. Practice walking pigeon-toed with toes curled. Try picking up and carrying small rocks, marbles, or pencils with toes.

DUAL CONTESTS FOR WEBELOS SCOUTS

A good athlete keeps in shape by exercising. It can be more fun when you do this with a friend. Dual contests give you the chance to test your strength and your ability to react quickly. If you should lose, find out what your friend is doing that is better. Then practice up. Maybe you can win next time. Whether you swim or race or play games, dual contests are all good conditioners.

For the dual contests on these pages, you will need only simple things, such as broomsticks, ropes, and belts. You can try these almost anytime and anywhere.

If the other boy is a little stronger, so much the better. This will make you try harder. Keep practicing the exercises so you can do better next time.

INDIAN ARM WRESTLE: Try to force your opponent's hand to the ground or raise his elbow. You must do this without moving your own elbow. Try changing hands.

STICK FIGHT: Grip the stick firmly—left hand up, right hand down. Try to force the left end of the stick to the ground. Repeat several times.

BACK PULL: Stand back to back. Lock hands over shoulders. Try to pull your opponent off his feet. Then carry him back to the finish line.

STICK PULL: Sit on the ground, facing each other. Put the soles of your shoes together. To win, pull your opponent forward to his feet.

SHOULDER PUSH: Face each other 6 feet apart. Lean forward with hands on other's shoulders. Try to push opponent back at least three steps.

BELT TUG: Fasten belts together. Place them as loops around your heads. Try to pull the belt off your opponent's head without knees or hands leaving the ground.

PULL APART: Sit foot to foot with hands locked and legs spread wide apart. Try to pull the other up. The winner is on his back at end.

DUCK FIGHT: Grasp ankles in low squat position. Butt the other with head or shoulders. Winner must force opponent to let go or fall.

CHEST PUSH: Start contest between two lines, 10 feet apart. Push chest against chest, arms out, hands touching. Winner must force opponent back over line.

INDIAN LEG WRESTLE: Lie on your backs, head to feet, and link inside elbows. Raise inside legs three times. On the third count, try to catch opponent's heel and flip him.

61

ATHLETE
SCOREBOARD

Requirements

CITIZEN

In the Cub Scout Promise you say you will do your duty to your country. This means being a good citizen.

As a Cub Scout, you have learned good citizenship in several ways. You helped others with Good Turns. You worked together with your den and pack. As a Webelos Scout, and later as a Scout, you will do even more. You will help others more than ever before.

You are a citizen of your town, of your state, and of the United States. Just how did you become a citizen? You became one when you were born if your parents were citizens. Perhaps you are from another country. Then you became a citizen of the United States when your parents were naturalized. That means that they studied about the United States. Then they went to the courthouse in your town. They pledged allegiance to this country, just as you pledge allegiance to the flag.

But being a citizen is not the same as being a good citizen. On the following pages you will find things that a good citizen knows and does.

To earn this badge, you must RECORD the things you do in a notebook. You must DO three things listed below. In addition, DO any five on the next page. You may work on the tests at home with mother and dad. The things you learn from them will be very helpful to all of you.

DO ALL OF THESE:
- The Declaration of Independence says "...that all men are created equal." Tell what you think this means in America today (or what it means to you).
- Know the historical background of the poem "The Star-Spangled Banner." Write about this story in your notebook.
- Know the names of the president and vice president of the United States. Know the name of your state governor and the head of your local government. List them in your notebook. Put in pictures of your national and state capitols.

DO ANY FIVE OF THE FOLLOWING:

- Tell about another boy who you think is a good citizen. Tell what he does that makes you think he is.

- In your notebook, write a short story of not less than 50 words about a former U.S. president. Or, write about some other great American man or woman living today.

- List five people who you think are good citizens. They can be from any country. Tell why you chose each of them.

- Tell why we have laws. Tell why you think it is important to obey the law. Tell about three laws that you obeyed this week.

- Tell three things that the U.S. Government does to help you or your family. Tell three things that your state or local government does for you. Tell what you do for your government.

- Tell why we have a government. Find out some ways your family helps pay for government.

- List six ways in which your country helps or works with other nations.

- Name three organizations (not churches) in your area that help people. Tell something about what one of these organizations does.

- Alone or with your Webelos den do a special Good Turn. Help your church, synagogue, school, neighborhood, or town. Tell what you did.

66

THE DECLARATION
OF INDEPENDENCE

Two hundred years ago England ruled most of the settled parts of this country. The English king did not always treat his American colonists fairly, especially in taxing them. This angered the Americans more and more. Finally, in April 1775 war began.

Leaders from the 13 colonies had been meeting in Philadelphia since 1774. In the summer of 1776 they decided on freedom from England once and for all. So a committee, headed by Thomas Jefferson, wrote the Declaration of Independence. It said that from then on the Colonies would be free to rule themselves.

One of the Declaration's greatest sentences says that all men are created equal. This is very important. It was the first time any government had said that no citizen was better than another.

"All men are created equal." What did the leaders mean when they wrote that? Did they think that no one is smarter than anyone else? Can everyone run as fast or jump as high as the next person?

In saying "All men are created equal," they meant something else. No one was to have special privileges. Every citizen in the United States would have the same rights. Everyone would be taxed alike. Each man would be treated the same as his neighbor in a court of law.

What does it mean today? Just this—that you must be treated just like anyone else anywhere in our country. You cannot be arrested without reason. Our government cannot give some other citizen any right that you don't have.

It does not mean that anybody has to like you or pay any special attention to you. And it doesn't mean that you can do anything you want to.

Think over what it means to you and write your ideas in your notebook.

"THE STAR-SPANGLED BANNER"

Every good citizen knows "The Star-Spangled Banner," our national anthem. If you have forgotten it, get your *Wolf Cub Scout Book*. It's on page 134.

Francis Scott Key, lawyer-poet from Georgetown (near Washington, D.C.), wrote the poem in 1814. Our country was fighting England in the War of 1812. English ships fired on Fort McHenry, near Baltimore, Md. The fort returned fire. Key was on an English ship. He had come earlier, under a truce flag, to rescue Dr. Beans of Baltimore. The battle lasted into the night. Anxiously they awaited sunrise. The Stars and Stripes still waved proudly. The fort held out! Meanwhile, Key had begun the poem in the light of the rocket's red glare. He finished it the next night. It was later set to music.

GOVERNMENT AND YOU

A good citizen knows what his government is doing. He tries to find out what is happening. He reads newspapers. He watches and listens to the news on television and radio.

You may not understand everything you read or hear. Talk it over with your parents.

Learn the names of the president and vice president of our country. Find out who the governor of your state is. Learn who is head of the government for your city, town, or county. Ask your parents what the duties of each one are.

WHAT IS A GOOD CITIZEN?

How can you tell whether a person is a good citizen? Here are a few signs:

- He obeys the law. If he thinks a law is wrong, he tries to have it changed. He does this by telling the people who are elected to make laws.
- He respects the rights of others. He does not try to get special privileges for himself.
- He tries to be fair and honest with everyone.
- He tries to make his country or town a better place.

- If in school, he "does his best" to learn all he can about his country.
- If grown up, he learns all that he can about his government. Then he votes on election day.

Do you know a boy who you think is a good citizen? What about a former president or some other great American? Can you find out something about him to show that he is a good citizen? Do you know of five people from any country who are fine citizens?

Answer yes to those questions and you can do the first three optional requirements. Your parents or teacher may be able to suggest some names to you.

WHY WE NEED
LAWS AND GOVERNMENT

We have said that a good citizen obeys the law. But why have laws or a government?

What would it be like if we did not have either one? In the first place, if there were no laws, everyone could do anything he wanted. Does that sound wonderful? What would it mean? Think about it a minute. If someone stole your bike, could you get it back? Probably not, especially if the thief were bigger than you. It would mean that if someone killed another person, he would not be arrested for it.

We have laws so that people can be safe. We have laws so that people can enjoy what they own.

What if there was no government? What would that mean? It would mean there would be no policemen to see that the laws are obeyed. There would be no firemen to help save your house if it caught fire. There would be no Army to fight for our country if it was attacked. Government takes care of all those things and many more.

LAWS YOU OBEY

You obey laws every day of your life. Perhaps you didn't even know that you are doing it. Here are some times when you obey laws:

- When you are riding your bike and stop for a red traffic light.

- When you go to school. Your state has a law saying that you must attend school unless you are sick.

- When you follow the school crossing guard's orders.

- When you are walking and cross streets only at corners when it is safe.

- When you take good care of your pet. There is a law stating that you must not mistreat or harm animals.

- When you go fishing with your dad and stop at the number of fish allowed. A law sets that limit.

These are just a few examples. Talk it over with your parents and see what other laws you obey.

HOW GOVERNMENT HELPS YOU

People elected by your parents and other adult citizens make our laws. Some of these people are elected to make laws for the whole United States. Others do this only for your state, city, or county.

These people try to make laws that will help you to live better. There are also laws to protect your rights. The U.S. Government uses your parents' taxes to help your family and others by:

- Running the post office, so that your mail is sent and delivered safely.
- Building big national parks for your enjoyment.
- Protecting natural resources, such as forests, streams, and wildlife, so that you can enjoy them.
- Helping your parents to find a job when they need one.
- Making sure that the food and drugs that you buy are clean and safe.
- Building highways so that you can travel quickly and safely.

Your state government helps your family too. Here are just a few of the ways:

- Sets the standards for your town's schools. Helps pay for them.
- Issues drivers' licenses and license plates so your parents can have and use their car.
- Builds roads between towns in the many parts of the state.

Your local government makes and enforces the laws for your city, town, or county. Here are some of the things it does for your family:

- Pays policemen to protect and help you and your family.
- Pays firemen to guard against fires.
- Builds streets in your community.
- Builds sewers to carry away the wastes from your house.
- Lights your streets at night.
- Builds playgrounds for you.

The governments of our country, your state, and your community do other things for people. Talk about these with your parents. All of these things cost money—a lot of money. The government gets most of the money to pay for these services from taxes. Your parents can tell you what taxes your family pays.

You and your family can do other things for your government besides paying taxes. Talk about these with your dad.

CITIZENSHIP IN THE WORLD

Our country is full of good citizens. And it is a good citizen, too, because it helps other countries. The United States is the richest country in the world. Some nations are so poor that many children go hungry. There are no schools for them. Our country tries to help other nations in several ways. Here are some:

- By giving them food and services or lending money at little cost.
- By sending Peace Corps workers to help build roads, bridges, and factories. They also teach in the schools and show farmers the best way to grow crops.

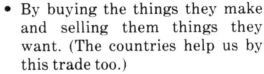

- By buying the things they make and selling them things they want. (The countries help us by this trade too.)
- By sending doctors, scientists, and engineers to work in other countries.

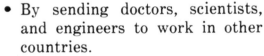

- By bringing students from other countries to the United States to study.

These are things that our government does. Americans themselves help in other ways too. For example, there is CARE. Our citizens give money to CARE. CARE sends food and clothing to poor people in other countries. Of course, there is our own World Friendship Fund. Cub Scouts, Scouts, and Explorers can help other Scout groups around the world. They do this by their gifts to the fund.

CITIZENSHIP IN YOUR TOWN

You have seen how good citizenship works allover the world. But remember that it starts very near you. This is right in your own hometown.

Many people in your community show good citizenship by working without pay and giving money to a lot of groups that do things for others. Here are a few of these groups your town may have:

- Volunteer fire department
- Rescue squad
- Red Cross
- Recreation association
- United Way
- Humane society to take care of lost pets
- Salvation Army
- And last but not least, the Boy Scouts of America

CITIZENSHIP AND YOU

Yes, citizenship starts close to home. In fact, it begins with YOU. Already you have seen that a good citizen obeys the law. He respects the rights of others. He always tries to be fair. But he does even more than that. He does a Good Turn to help other people whenever possible. What can you and your den do to help your church, synagogue, school, or town? Talk about this with your Webelos leader.

CITIZEN SCOREBOARD

Requirements

Approved
by

DO ALL OF THESE:

⊙ The Declaration of Independence says "...that all men are created equal." Tell what you think this means in America today (or what it means to you). 68

Fail

⊙ Know the historical background of the poem "The Star-Spangled Banner." Write about this story in your notebook. 69

R. Flood

⊙ Know the names of the president and vice president of the United States. Know the name of your state governor and the head of your local government. List them in your notebook. Put in pictures of your national and state capitols. 70

R. Flood

AND DO FIVE:

• Tell about another boy who you think is a good citizen. Tell what he does that makes you think he is. 71

• In your notebook, write a short story of not less than 50 words about a former U.S. president. Or, write about some other great American man or woman living today.

- List five people who you think are good citizens. They can be from any country. Tell why you chose each of them.   71

- Tell why we have laws. Tell why you think it is important to obey the law. Tell about three laws that you obeyed this week.   72

- Tell three things that the U.S. Government does to help you or your family. Tell three things that your state or local government does for you. Tell what you do for your government.   74

- Tell why we have a government. Find out some ways your family helps pay for government.   75

- List six ways in which your country helps or works with other nations.   76

- Name three organizations (not churches) in your area that help people. Tell something about what one of these organizations does.   77

- Alone or with your Webelos den do a special Good Turn. Help your church, synagogue, school, neighborhood, or town. Tell what you did.   77

79

CRAFTSMAN

Do you want to be a doctor, a carpenter, a lawyer, or a mechanic? It doesn't matter—you will want to know how to make things with tools.

Some men use tools in their regular work. Others enjoy hobbies such as working with wood, leather, or clay. As a Cub Scout, you learned how to use tools. You have made things with them. Now, as a Webelos Scout, you should be a lot better at it. You should be able to make harder things.

For this activity badge, you will be making useful things. You will also learn how to make them look nice. There are plans here for toys, tie racks, bookmarks, and letter holders. Try them all. Then make something of your own design.

DO THE FOLLOWING:

- **Using hand tools, make two wooden toys.**
- **Cut out four different things that will require the use of a jigsaw or coping saw such as:**

Bookrack	**Note pad holder**
Shelf	**Toolbox**
Bulletin board	**Towel rack**
Weather vane	**Recipe holder**
Tie rack	**Lampstand**
Letter holder	

Put them together and paint or stain them.

AND COMPLETE ONE OF THESE:

- **Make four useful things in leather. Design these yourself. Include cutting, tooling, and lacing.**
- **Make four useful things of tin. Cut, join, and rivet metal in making these.**

MATERIALS AND METHODS

Practice using your materials and tools until you know them well.

Keep your costs down. Use scrap material. Protect your tools. Put them back in place. Clean up when you are through working.

Keep your workshop in order. A clean bench makes a better place to work.

WOODWORKING

A B

SLOT FOR STRING

HINGE BACK COVER

FASTEN FRONT LEGS SECURELY

PEDRO

With the help of the drawing, it shouldn't be too hard to make Pedro. He nods his head and kicks his heels. Pedro is made of light wood and has two sides. One of them has been taken off so you can see how to string the pendulum.

1. Pivot on either a small bolt and nut or nail. It should be loose enough to swing freely.
2. String to pendulum. Test it before putting on other side of burro.

Longer strings in a longer box cause a slower and longer movement. You can make other things like a clown, a bear, or a lion.

THE ECCENTRIC WHEEL

This is an old idea in toy making. When this method is used, the head bobs in and out. See how many different toys you can make using this idea.

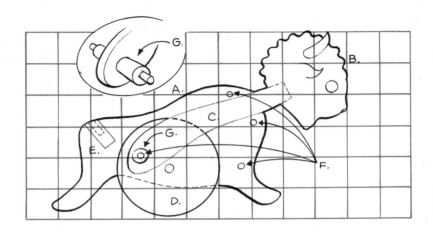

A. Body—make two 3/8 by 12 inches

B. Head—make one 3/4 by 5 inches

C. Neck—make one 1/4-inch plywood 2 by 10 inches

D. Wheels—make two 3/4-inch plywood 5-3/4 inch diameter

E. Block—make one 3/4 by 1-3/4 by 3-1/4 inches

F. Dowels—make four 3/8 by 4 inches

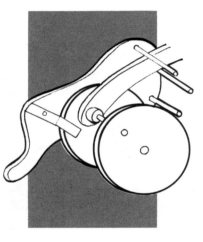

G. Dowels—make two 3/4 by 1-5/16 inches—hole through center 7/16 inch

Fasten the wheels to the inside of the body pieces with short bolts. Put the 3/8-inch dowel in the end of the neck. Slide on the 3/4-inch dowels and put ends in the wheels. Finish your work. Put handle in block.

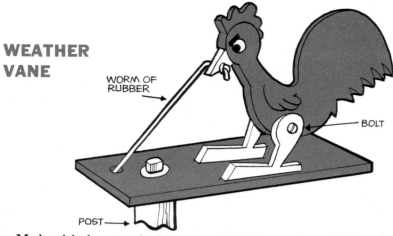

WEATHER VANE

WORM OF RUBBER

BOLT

POST

Make bird out of thin wood. Bolt on legs. Fasten bird to 1- by 6- by 12-inch board. Fasten board to post with washers and bolt so board can turn.

"Worm" is a piece of inner tube or wire.

LETTER HOLDER

Draw the duck on a 6- by 8-inch piece of ½-inch plywood. Make sure that you draw his feet and outspread wings.

Cut them out. Sand and paint them. Fasten them to a piece of 1- by 2- by 6-inch wood as shown.

2"

6"

TIE RACK

Drill holes for dowels in a piece of 1- by 2-inch wood. Cut end pieces from 1- by 2-inch lumber and the back of ¼-inch plywood. Sand and paint all pieces. When dry, put them together. Cut dowels. Sand one end of each piece. Drive rough ends into holes.

TOOLS FOR YOUR WORKSHOP

Choose your tools carefully. Add to them slowly. Buy only good tools. You may have to wait longer and save a little more money. A good tool is worth it.

Here is a list of tools needed to work with wood:

- **Nail hammer**
- **Nail set**
- **Pair combination pliers**
- **Screwdriver**
- **Combination square**

- **Crosscut saw**
- **Ripsaw**
- **Hacksaw**
- **Plane**
- **Rachet brace**
- **Set of auger bits**
- **Folding rule**

- **Hand drill**
- **Set of bits**
- **Level**
- **Several C-clamps**
- **Set pocket chisels**
- **Combination oilstone**

Add to this list by getting different sizes and kinds of each item.

One of the first power tools that you will want is a jigsaw. Here again, shop for a good one. The saw shown on this page is a real strong little tool. It is fine for use in an apartment, workshop, or garage. This jigsaw is very safe to use. There is no vibration, and it runs quietly.

The base has four rubber suction feet that stick to any smooth, solid surface. If you live in an apartment or haven't room for a workshop, it is great. When you are finished with your work, put it away on a closet shelf. It takes up very little space.

Your local Scout outfitter, the place where you got your uniform, probably has them for sale.

LEATHERWORK

For your first project, make a bookmark.

1. **CHOOSE YOUR DESIGN:** Choose a simple design to begin with. It should have straight lines and free-flowing curves.

2. **TRACE THE DESIGN:** Place a piece of transparent paper over your design. Trace the design on your paper.

3. **CUT LEATHER TO SIZE NEEDED:** Place leather, finished side up, on a piece of pressed board. Lay a straightedge—a yardstick is good —along the line. With a sharp knife, cut along the straightedge. Be sure that your fingers are out of the way. Make your cut with one stroke.

4. **WET THE LEATHER:** Lay the bookmark on your bench with the flesh side up. Dampen the whole thing with a squeezed-out, clean cloth, pad, or sponge. Too much water will discolor the leather.

5. **TRACE THE DESIGN ON THE LEATHER:** Place the tracing on the smooth side of the leather. Be sure that it is centered. Fold the edges of the paper under the leather. Use tape on the smooth side of the leather. Don't use paperclips. They might mark the leather. Place the dampened bookmark, smooth side up, on a solid surface. Use a tracing tool to transfer the design to the leather. Use just enough pressure to make a clear line on the leather.

6. **DAMPEN FOR TOOLING:** Remove the pattern paper. Wet the leather again — just enough to darken the tooled line.

7. **TOOL DESIGN IN BOOKMARK:**
Use the curved point of the spoon to make the lines deeper. Hold it like a pencil and draw the tool toward you as you push down.

When working around a point, hold the tool straighter. Use a straightedge to tool all straight lines. In making a square corner, turn the leather around. Push the tool into the corner. Go over and over the design until it is well tooled in.

8. **STIPPLE THE BACKGROUND:** This is lowering the background by hitting it over and over with a blunt tool. Be sure you don't hit the design.

9. **FRINGE THE END:** Divide the width of the bookmark into 1/8- or ¼-inch spaces. Use the straightedge and the pointed edge of your modeling tool. Put the leather on the cutting block. With knife and straightedge, make 2-inch-long cuts as shown.

10. **STAIN EDGES:** With a leather dye and striping brush, stain all cut edges of the leather. Put on dye from sides of bristles. The tip of the brush should be below the flesh side of the leather.

11. **CREASE THE EDGE:** Draw the creaser back and forth along the edge of the bookmark. Use firm, even pressure.

12. **CLEAN THE BOOKMARK:** With a damp cloth, put on a little saddle soap. Let it dry. Polish with a soft, dry pad.

If you are new at leathercraft, start with something simple. Work up from there. Later, you may want to make your own designs.

Take care of your tools. Have a place for each one. Keep it there. Then edges won't become damaged. A dull knife can cause you real trouble in leathercraft.

USING TEMPLATES

You'll find using patterns will be helpful in laying out your work. These are called templates. They save time and material.

There are many places to find help. Check your craft magazines, the yellow pages in the telephone book, and the library. Get names of leatherwork companies. Write for their catalogs. The price lists of tools and leather often have things to make. They include:

Luggage tags	Billfolds	Scuffles
Key cases	Pocket secretary	Album
Eyeglass cases	Coin purse	Moccasins
Watch straps	Belts	Notebook
Checkbook covers	Picture frames	Purse
Book cover	Drawstring purse	Wastebasket

METAL WORKING

LAYOUT BOARD

Get a piece of ¾-inch plywood, 12 by 18 inches in size. Fasten a ruler on one end of it. It is handy for measurements. Laying out your pattern, you get a square edge to run your triangle along.

To get the most metal from a can, take off both ends. With tin snips, cut along both sides of the seam. Open the can. Flatten it. Then cut off the rims on each edge.

Place the tin on your layout board. Smooth it out with the end of a stick or the head of your hammer. Rub it—don't pound. Pounding makes dents which have to be smoothed out later.

TO MAKE A SIMPLE BEND

Mark the metal where the bend is to be. Put a block of wood in a vise. Lay the "bending line" along the sharp edge of the wood. Hold it firmly in place. Bend down the metal that sticks out to form a right angle.

Fold this piece over on itself and form a simple joint.

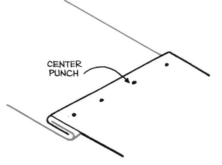

CENTER PUNCH

To join two pieces of metal together, make a joint like this on each piece. Pull them together. Flatten the joint. Then set it with a center punch.

PUNCHES

Punches for different size holes can be made from nails. Simply cut off the pointed ends. To make a hole in metal, put it on the end of a wooden block. Set the punch in place and tap lightly. Check to be sure that it is in the right place. Put the punch back. Hit it hard. Turn the metal over to flatten the burr.

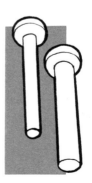

TO RIVET

Punch or drill holes in metal to be joined. Put in the rivet. Pound the end to force the metal down. Pound straight down to spread the rivet in the hole. Round off the rivet head with a ball peen hammer.

TOOLS FOR METAL WORK

MACHINIST'S VISE: A "must" tool in the craft shop.

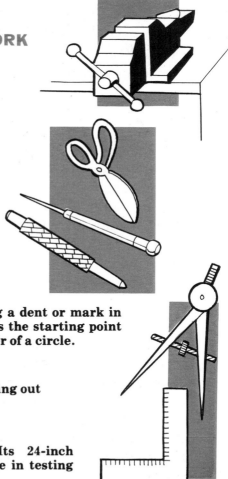

TIN SHEARS: Buy a size that you can handle easily. The metal you work with isn't thick. So, the shears don't have to be large.

SCRATCH AWL: For marking lines on metals.

CENTER PUNCH: For making a dent or mark in the surface of metal. For use as the starting point for a drill. For making the center of a circle.

MARKING GAUGE: For marking out width of strips.

CARPENTER'S SQUARE: Its 24-inch blade is used as a straightedge in testing and layout work.

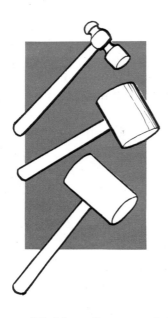

BALL PEEN HAMMER: An all-purpose hammer in the craft shop. Comes in 8- and 16-ounce sizes.

MALLETS AND SOFT-FACED HAMMERS: For striking the metal when working it.

RIVETING HAMMER: Especially for riveting. Comes in 4- to 12-ounce sizes.

Making four useful things of metal gives you a wide choice. You have to be quite good to make these candleholders. You will have to cut, shape, and rivet.

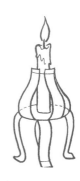

Choose tin cans with color for more beauty. Put one color against the other. In the case of the leaves, cut them down to the line. Then twist every other one once to get a two-color effect.

CRAFTSMAN SCOREBOARD

Requirements

Approved
by

Page

DO THESE:

_____

• Using hand tools, make two wooden toys.
• Cut out four different things that will require the use of a jigsaw or coping saw such as:

Bookrack	Note pad holder
Shelf	Toolbox
Bulletin board	Towel rack
Weather vane	Recipe holder
Tie rack	Lampstand
Letter holder	

Put them together and paint
_____
or stain them.

AND DO ONE OF THESE:

aug '81
Leather
done @ camp

_____

• Make four useful things in leather. Design these yourself. Include cutting, tooling, and lacing.   86

_____

• Make four useful things of tin. Cut, join, and rivet metal in making these.   89

ENGINEER

There are almost as many kinds of engineers as there are jobs to be done. They take the raw materials of nature and change them for the use of mankind.

A civil engineer draws up the plans for a job. He oversees all the work on it. He also designs plants that make our water safe to drink.

A mechanical engineer designs machines in a factory. Chemical engineers test new processes and check old ones in a chemical plant. An electrical engineer plans new circuits and directs the workers in an electrical plant.

There are engineers in aerospace work, industry, agriculture, and many other areas. The engineering field gets larger every year. More and more engineers are needed.

In earning your Engineering badge, you will learn many useful things. You will need them for merit badge work as a Scout.

COMPLETE FIVE OF THE FOLLOWING:

- List 10 different things engineers do.
- Visit a construction job. Look at a set of plans. Tell your Webelos den leader about these. (Get permission before your visit.)
- Measure the length of a property line. Explain how property lines are determined.
- Make a drawing of how electricity gets to your house.
- Make drawings of three kinds of bridges. Explain them.
- Make and show how a block and tackle works.
- Build and show how a catapult works.
- Draw a floor plan of your house. Include doors, windows, and stairways.

Engineering can be put into three lists:

DESIGN: Machines; chemical processes; buildings; highways; water, power, and communications systems.

SUPERVISE: Manufacturing; building of bridges, dams, buildings, transportation facilities, and vehicles.

INVESTIGATE: Traffic problems; water and air pollution; waste disposal; power distribution; need for river flood control.

SURVEYING LAND

A deed is a paper describing a piece of property. It uses fixed points for this such as a nail set in concrete. To check a boundary line, measure the distances and angles. Set points along the line described.

BLOCK AND TACKLE

A block and tackle is a set of pulleys and rope. It is used to lift heavy weights easily.

The rope is threaded through the pulleys as shown. The load is divided equally on all parts of the rope. The complete weight is moved easily. Only a small part of the force needed for lifting without tackle is used.

Get some small double and single pulleys. Rig them in the ways shown. Try each one. Decide which one has the greatest lift.

Luff

Single Whip

Two Fold

Runner

Spanish Burton

Gun Tackle

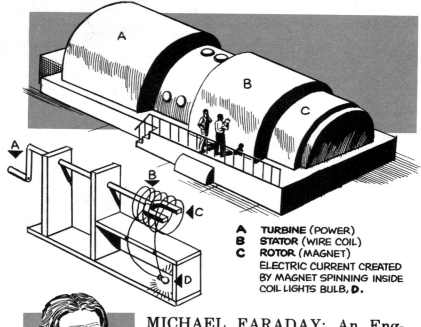

A **TURBINE** (POWER)
B **STATOR** (WIRE COIL)
C **ROTOR** (MAGNET)
ELECTRIC CURRENT CREATED
BY MAGNET SPINNING INSIDE
COIL LIGHTS BULB, **D.**

MICHAEL FARADAY: An English physicist who lived in the 1800's. He discovered that electricity can be made by breaking up a magnetic field. You can make electricity with a simple generator.

Turbines are like huge waterwheels. They are spun around by water, steam, or other power. These turbines are hooked up with generators that spin rapidly. They stir up electrons that move over the wires as electricity.

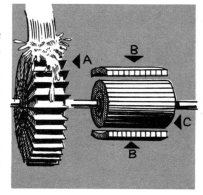

The electricity is sent over wires to a boos
tion. There it is raised from about 12,000 v
about 220,000 or more volts. A transformer doe
Transformers can be used to make the voltage ....s.
This is called stepping it down. They can step it up
higher as well.

BOOSTER
STATION

A simple transformer is an
iron frame (called the core)
and two pieces of wire wound
around it. There are more
windings on one side than on
the other. Voltage is raised or
lowered by the direction of the
electricity flow.

REDUCING
STATION

HOW ELECTRICITY GETS TO YOUR HOUSE

Try to trace electricity
from where it is made to
your home. First water,
steam, or other power turns
a turbine. This turbine spins
a generator. The generator
makes electricity.

Electricity moves along
wires like water running
through a pipe. We need a
big enough supply to meet
our needs. The wires must be
big enough to carry it.

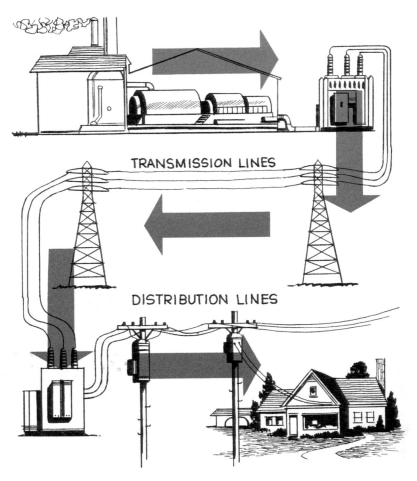

TRANSMISSION LINES

DISTRIBUTION LINES

Electricity is made in a large plant called a power station. It must get to your home without too much leaking from the wires. Raising the voltage at a transformer station near the powerhouse does this. A high-tension line carries the high-voltage electricity to your town. There it is reduced by other transformers. Then it goes by lower voltage wires to homes.

SAFETY RULES

Even low voltage is strong enough to kill you. It can give you a hard shock or a bad burn. For your safety's sake, know your betters:

- Better not touch a switch with wet hands or while standing on a damp floor.

- Better use only one thing at one outlet. Overloading causes fires.

- Better not put electric wires under rugs and carpets. Walking on wires wears off the insulation. This causes shorts.

- Better use the right fuse in your fuse box.

- Better not touch anything electrical while taking a bath.

- Better not get under a tree during a thunderstorm.

- Better get out of the swimming pool or lake during a heavy storm.

BRIDGES

The best way to learn about bridges is to study the way they are made. Then build some yourself. Not great big bridges, of course, but models, just the way engineers do. You can use bricks, wooden blocks, and heavy paper.

Start with a plank bridge. Set up the two bricks. Lay a heavy piece of paper on them to go over "the river" beneath. What happens when you put one of your toy cars on the bridge?

What would you do to hold up the middle? Putting the wooden block under it helps. This is called a pier bridge. Take another piece of paper and fold the sides up 1 inch. Set this on the bricks. How much weight does this hold? More than the plain piece of paper? This is called a beam bridge. You may have seen them under the railroad tracks. They hold up a heavy weight over a short distance.

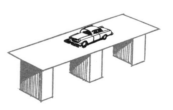

Bend a piece of heavy paper so that it forms an arch. Slip it in between the two bricks. Set a piece of heavy paper on top of it and the bricks. This is called an arch bridge. Does it hold more weight than the others?

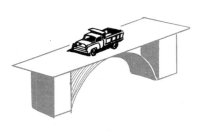

Engineers know about shapes and how much each one will hold up. Make a square out of four straws. Do this by sticking a pin through them near each end. Stand it up. Is it rigid? Does it want to fold up?

Make a triangle out of these straws. Does it move out of shape? In building very long bridges, engineers use a whole row of triangles. These are called truss bridges and cantilever bridges.

Suspension cable bridges are the largest. Can you give some examples?

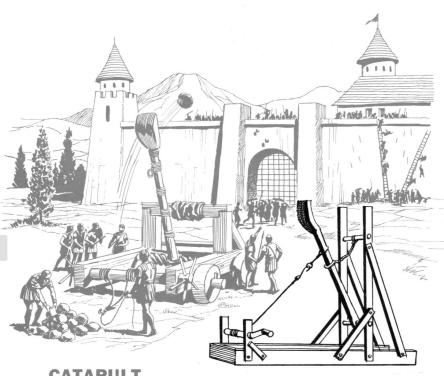

CATAPULT

Study the catapult. Figure out how they were used in throwing rocks over city walls in ancient wars. Soldiers loaded rocks into the cradle or box of the catapult. How did they get the arm down to do this? How did they let it go so that it would fly up with a snap?

A simple mousetrap is a form of catapult. At least it can be used to throw objects across the room.

You need a strong spring or rubber bands to snap the arm back into position. A crank to wind the arm down into firing position is also needed. You should have a way to let go of the arm instantly. Can you make a model that will work?

ENGINEER
SCOREBOARD

FORESTER

What's a tree?

Does that sound like a silly question? You'll answer, "Why, it's that big tall thing over there with all the leaves."

Of course it is. It also is a great sample of God's handiwork. It is one of the most useful things on earth for man.

A forester is a man who knows forestry. That is the care and growing of trees. As a Scout, you will spend a lot of time in the forest. You will find it more fun if you learn more about the trees around you.

In earning your Forester badge, you'll get started as a good woodsman. You will learn to know the kinds of trees. You will find out what sort of wood they make. You will learn how to plant a tree and how it lives and grows.

When you know this, you will be a better Scout. This is because you always will be among friends —both boys and trees.

COMPLETE FIVE
OF THE FOLLOWING:

- Identify six forest trees. Tell what useful things come from them.

- Identify six forest plants that are useful to wildlife. Tell what animals use them and for what.

- Make a poster showing the life history of a forest tree.

- Make a chart showing how water and minerals in the soil help a tree grow.

- Collect pieces of three kinds of wood used for building houses.

- Plant 20 forest tree seedlings. Care for them for a month.

- Describe the harm caused by wildfires. Tell how you may help prevent wildfire.

- Make a map of the United States. Show the kinds of forests growing in the different parts of the U.S.A. Tell what important things made of wood come from each part.

A forester must know the names of the trees with which he is working. He knows that some trees are better for timber than others. Some are more useful for paper pulp. Some provide more food for wildlife.

Most trees grow best in certain kinds of places. To improve forests over the years, a forester must know trees and what they need to grow. He must know their wood characteristics.

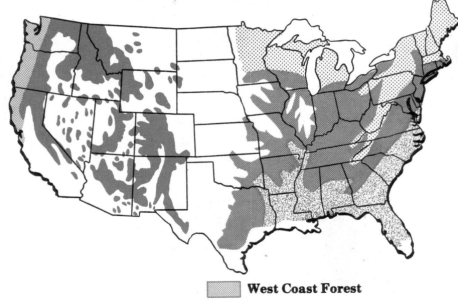

PRINCIPAL FOREST AREAS OF THE UNITED STATES

West Coast Forest

Western Forest

Northern Forest

Central Hardwood Forest

Southern Forest

109

The main forest product is wood. Wood is one of the world's most useful things. Man depends upon it in his home, business, and daily living. Forests protect our watersheds and prevent erosion.

Learn to identify trees in your backyard, your neighborhood, and your city park. You should know the trees that are most common where you live. You may have to hunt to find some of them, but keep looking. It's worth the effort.

Many birds and other animals count on forest plants for food. This food could be in the form of seeds, nuts, flowers, bark, or wood.

Can you name five other plants that support animal life?

Trees are the world's largest plants. They reach from 20 to over 300 feet tall. They have three parts. The roots are first. These feed the tree by taking up water and minerals from the ground. The trunk is second. It holds up the crown. It carries minerals and water to the crown. The crown is the third part. It acts as a factory. Its leaves change minerals and water to food needed for growth.

HOW A
TREE GROWS

CROWN: Trees get bigger each year by adding a new growth of twigs. This growth comes from young cells in the buds at the ends of the twigs.

TRUNK: This part holds up the top. It produces most of the useful wood.

ROOTS: They anchor the tree. Roots soak up water with minerals and nitrogen needed to make food. They hold the soil against erosion. A layer of growth cells at root tips makes new tissue each year.

THE INSIDE STORY OF A TREE

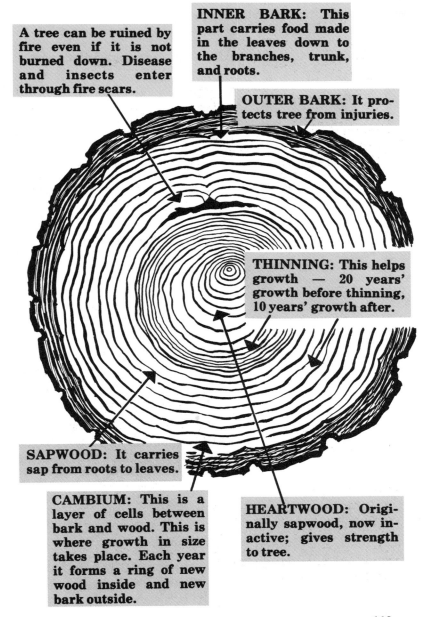

A tree can be ruined by fire even if it is not burned down. Disease and insects enter through fire scars.

INNER BARK: This part carries food made in the leaves down to the branches, trunk, and roots.

OUTER BARK: It protects tree from injuries.

THINNING: This helps growth — 20 years' growth before thinning, 10 years' growth after.

SAPWOOD: It carries sap from roots to leaves.

CAMBIUM: This is a layer of cells between bark and wood. This is where growth in size takes place. Each year it forms a ring of new wood inside and new bark outside.

HEARTWOOD: Originally sapwood, now inactive; gives strength to tree.

TREE PLANTING

- **Carry seedlings in a bucket or box. Keep the roots damp.**

- **Plant them at least 6 feet apart.**

- **Dig the holes deep enough to let the roots spread out and downward.**

- **Stamp the soil down firmly around the roots to prevent air pockets. If you don't, the roots will dry out and the tree will probably die.**

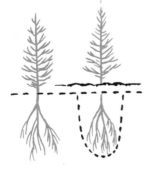

- **A tree should be straight up and even with the ground. It should not be sunk in or mounded up above the ground.**

- **A tree should be planted so that the old groundline is below ground level. (The groundline is the dark mark on the trunk.) It should be about ¼ inch below.**

PREVENT WILDFIRES

Wildfire in a forest does much more than destroy trees. It also destroys food and cover for wildlife. Sometimes it destroys the animals themselves.

Wildfire burns the plant cover which protects the soil. Serious erosion often follows a fire. When soil and ashes wash into streams and lakes, good fishing may be spoiled. Campsites and other recreation areas may be destroyed by fire.

You can help prevent wildfire in these ways:

- Be extremely careful with any fire you build in the outdoors.

- Always build your fire in a safe place and watch it at all times.

- Do not leave a fire until it is cold out.

- You might see a small fire along the edge of a road or trail. Report it immediately to the nearest fire warden.

FORESTER SCOREBOARD

Requirements

Approved
by

DO FIVE:

- Identify six forest trees. Tell what useful things come from them.

- Identify six forest plants that are useful to wildlife. Tell what animals use them and for what.

- Make a poster showing the life history of a forest tree.

- Make a chart showing how water and minerals in the soil help a tree grow.

- Collect pieces of three kinds of wood used for building houses.

- Plant 20 forest tree seedlings. Care for them for a month.

- Describe the harm caused by wildfires. Tell how you may help prevent wildfire.

- Make a map of the United States. Show the kinds of forests growing in the different parts of the U.S.A. Tell what important things made of wood come from each part.

GEOLOGIST

A geologist is a person who studies the history of the earth and its life. His history books are rocks. He learns their uses and those of other minerals. He also studies volcanoes, geysers, and earthquakes. He is interested in learning as much as possible about how the earth is made.

Many of the things that he finds are useful to man. There are minerals, called ores, from which metals are made. He finds things like gypsum and sand, which are used in building. He looks for fuels like oil and natural gas, which are used in the heating of homes. He finds precious stones such as diamonds.

For this activity badge, you will learn many things that a geologist must know. You will find out how the earth is formed and what is in it. You'll learn what rock is and how it becomes sand, gravel, and clay.

You will find out what fossils are. You will learn what they can tell us about the earth millions of years ago. This beginning can help you to earn the Geology merit badge as a Scout.

DO FIVE OF THE FOLLOWING:

- Rocks and/or minerals are used in metals, glass, jewelry, road-building products, and fertilizer. Give examples.

- Collect five geologic specimens that have important uses to man.

- Make a scale of mineral hardness using things found at home. Show how to use the scale by finding the relative hardness of three samples.

- List some of the geologic materials used in building your home.

- Make a drawing that shows the cause of a volcano, a geyser, or an earthquake.

- Explain one way in which mountains are formed.

WHAT THE EARTH IS MADE OF

Are you a "pebble pup" or a real "rock hound"? It doesn't matter. Collecting and identifying rocks can be great fun. It might even lead to a job in geology.

The outdoors begins just outside your back door. Therefore, your own backyard is a good place to begin. Study the rocks that you pick up there or in the neighborhood. Using a guide to rocks and minerals, try to tell their names. As you learn, you are preparing for other adventures.

The whole earth's crust is made up of rocks or rock matter. You have seen great pieces of rock sticking out of the ground. Along the river there are solid rock cliffs. You've seen pictures of giant, bare mountain peaks of rock.

Some peaks are made up of layers of rock pushed up or on a slant. You may have noticed some. These rocks belong to one of the three main groups making up the earth's crust. They are sedimentary, igneous, and metamorphic rocks.

Scientists believe the first rock was made from melted rock, called magma.

Magma doesn't stand still. It flows sideways under the earth's crust. Sometimes it found a weak spot and broke through to form rolling hills or mountains. If there is a weakness in the earth's crust, magma may erupt as a volcano. Geologists believe that when magma and underground streams of water meet, steam forms. Then geysers, steam wells, and hot springs are formed.

IGNEOUS ROCK

Igneous rock is any rock made by the cooling of magma. It is not found in layers.

SEDIMENTARY ROCK

Sediment is gravel, sand, or clay laid down in riverbeds, ponds, lakes, and oceans. When sediment is under great pressure for millions of years, sedimentary rock is the result. It forms in layers, like a giant cake. If the sediment was sand, it became sandstone. Clay turned into shale. Small pebbles and sand formed conglomerate. Shells and skeletons made limestone.

METAMORPHIC ROCK

We might say that metamorphic rock is baked rock. Magma flowed through or over it, making it tough, hard, and glassy-looking. ("Meta" means changed and "morphic" means form.) Sedimentary limestone under great pressure and heat became marble. Sandstone turned into quartzite. Igneous granite changed into gneiss (pronounced "nice"). This is like what happens to clay heated in a kiln. It can become pottery or china.

Wind, water, sun, and cold are all very strong forces in the world. They can slowly break down any rock, no matter how strong. The result is sand, gravel, and clay. Soil forms when decayed plant and animal life are added through the years. It contains material ranging from tiny bacteria (plants) to worms and insects (animals). Plants for man and his animals will grow in soil if he takes care of it.

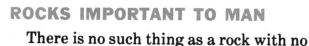

ROCKS IMPORTANT TO MAN

There is no such thing as a rock with no use at all. A rock that had no value yesterday may be worth a lot today. Perhaps someone discovered a new use for its mineral or an easier way to get it out. Maybe someday you will find a new source of minerals.

Minerals found in rocks furnish us with metals, fuels, and building materials.

Each mineral has its own physical and chemical makeup. Often it has its own crystal shape as well.

An ore is a mineral deposit from which one or more metals may be removed. Ores are found in all three kinds of rocks.

Useful minerals fall into three classes:

ORES

Iron	Tin	Platinum
Zinc	Mercury	Aluminum
Lead	Gold	Uranium
Copper	Silver	Magnesium

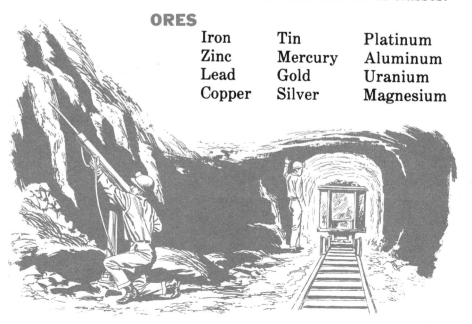

SOME NONMETALLIC PRODUCTS

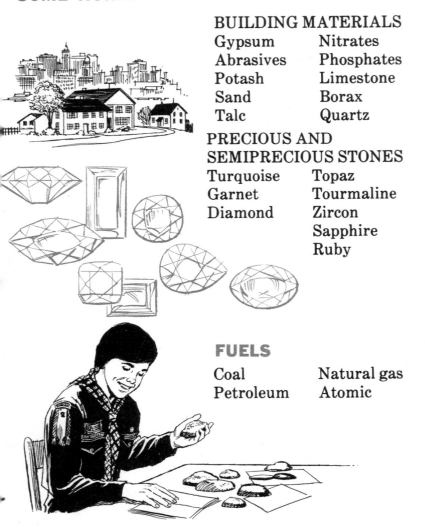

BUILDING MATERIALS

Gypsum	Nitrates
Abrasives	Phosphates
Potash	Limestone
Sand	Borax
Talc	Quartz

PRECIOUS AND SEMIPRECIOUS STONES

Turquoise	Topaz
Garnet	Tourmaline
Diamond	Zircon
	Sapphire
	Ruby

FUELS

Coal	Natural gas
Petroleum	Atomic

Learn to name some of these minerals by sight and by test. For this, you will need a good field guide to rocks and minerals. Check with your library.

Rocks and minerals, like human beings, have certain clues that show what they are. You can't name them by looks alone. Here are the test

COLOR CLUE: Scratch it on a plate of unglazed porcelain. Or use the back of a piece of tile.

LUSTER CLUE: How does it look when light is reflected from it? Is it shiny, dull, greasy, etc.?

CLEAVAGE CLUE: How does it split or break up? Crystals—how many sides? Does it powder? split in layers?

CHEMCIAL CLUE: Does it have any limestone? If a drop of vinegar bubbles on it, the answer is yes.

HARDNESS CLUE: How hard is it? See the hardness scale on the next page.

HARDNESS SCALE FOR MINERALS

Scale No.	Mineral Example	Scratch Test
1	Talc	Easily with fingernail
2	Gypsum	Barely with fingernail
3	Calcite	Barely with copper penny
4	Fluorite	Easily with knife blade
5	Apatite	Barely with knife blade
6	Feldspar	Not by blade; easily with glass
7	Quartz	Easily marks steel and hard glass
8	Topaz	Harder than common minerals
9	Corundum	Scratches topaz
10	Diamond	Scratches corundum; hardest mineral

GEOLOGIC MATERIALS
IN HOUSE CONSTRUCTION

Here are some of the geologic materials used in the building of a home. Maybe you can add others.

ORE	METAL	USE
Hematite Limonite Magnetite	Iron	Beams, girders, posts, nails, machines, screws
Azurite Malachite Chalcocite	Copper	Electric wiring, gutters, roofing, pipes
Galena	Lead	Pipes, paint, calking
Sphalerite	Zinc	Galvanizing pipe, sheet metal
Cinnabar	Mercury	Electric switches, thermostats
Bauxite	Aluminum	Siding, windows, doors, roofs
Quartz	Silicon	Glass
Kernite Borax	Boron	Glass
Limestone	Calcium	Cement, building stone

125

VOLCANOES

Volcanoes come in many sizes and shapes. They are simply holes in the ground through which streams of melted rock pour out of the earth. These streams are called lava. Lava changes the earth's shape as it flows. Cool lava becomes igneous rock.

In time, these rocks may build up into a mountain peak with a tube up the center. From this chimney comes the smoke, steam, and gas mixed with melted minerals.

As lava pours out, it spreads over the countryside and keeps building up. Geologists say that in some places this mineral rock may be thousands of feet deep.

Pumice stone (kitchen cleanser) is formed from the bubbling, foaming surface of melted lava.

Mount Capulin, a dead volcano in north-eastern New Mexico, is 8,215 feet above sea level. Wagon trains from Fort Dodge used it as a landmark. From its rim you can see parts of five states: New Mexico, Oklahoma, Texas, Kansas, and Colorado.

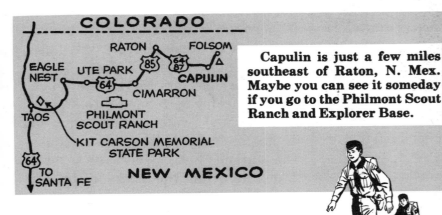

Capulin is just a few miles southeast of Raton, N. Mex. Maybe you can see it someday if you go to the Philmont Scout Ranch and Explorer Base.

Mount Capulin is one of the United States' largest recent cinder cones. It is one of the most perfectly shaped. It is more than 1,000 feet high from base to crater rim. The rim is 1 mile around. The center is 415 feet below the rim.

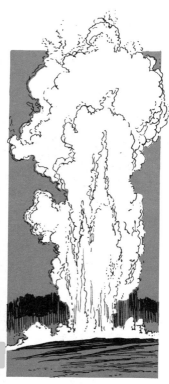

GEYSERS

Geologists believe that geysers are formed when melted rock meets underground water. This water is changed into steam quickly by the red-hot magma. The steam gathers in the geyser's tube. When enough pressure builds, it explodes and shoots up the spout. Then steam and boiling water blow into the air.

Old Faithful geyser is in the black sand basin of Yellowstone National Park. It shoots 100 to 150 feet into the air about every 70 to 90 minutes.

In some geysers, the steam pours out in a steady cloud. In others, the steam comes out in great amounts. This steam is piped to power plants and used to make electricity for use in our homes.

In other geysers there is so much water it can't be turned into steam. This heated water flows on and comes out as a hot spring. Because the water is hot, it dissolves several minerals from the rocks it passes over. Some of these mineral springs have become health resorts.

EARTHQUAKES

Standing upon the earth, you may think that it is quite solid. Yet it is not, really. Its crust is always changing. Thousands of years might pass, however, before there would be any difference in any one spot.

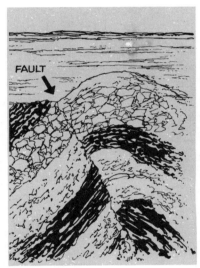

FAULT

Rocks in the earth's crust are under great pressure from other rocks on all sides. Sometimes they crack under the pressure. When they crack at once over a large area it is called an earthquake. A very bad earthquake may wreck a whole city.

An earthquake may happen very near the surface of the earth. Or it may be as much as 400 miles down. Scientists record earthquakes on a machine called a seismograph. It measures the vibrations.

HOW MOUNTAINS ARE FORMED

Mountains have been formed over millions of years. There are three basic ways this has been done:

The first way is volcanic action. Volcanoes and earthquakes prove that the earth is not fixed. It moves all the time, but the movement is so slow it seems that the earth is solid.

VOLCANIC ACTION

MOUNT HOOD, OREGON

EROSION

ADIRONDACK STATE PARK NEW YORK

UPLIFT FROM A BASIN

GLACIER NATIONAL PARK MONTANA

The second way is erosion. This is the wearing away and carrying off of material. Farm boys know about land erosion. Some mountains are made the same way. Small streams become big by heavy rains. They cut deeper and deeper. Finally, great valleys form and mountains stand where the land was once flat.

The third way is uplift from a basin. Uplift builds mountains by a whole series of events. Millions of years ago, the Rocky Mountains were a big flat under a shallow sea. Streams carried dirt and rocks into it. (Remember that this material is sediment.) This kept on for thousands of years. Finally, the basin floor became miles thick with sediment.

The basin's sides began pushing against this sediment, crushing it. This made the layers of rock and dirt fold. They began rising. Even as those layers rose, erosion began. This made mountains. This did not happen in a week or a year or even a hundred years. It took millions of years.

FOSSILS

There are usually fossils in sedimentary rock. Fossils are the signs of plant and animal life from long ago. They may be a shell's print or the skeleton of a fish or bird. They may be a dinosaur's track or a leaf or flower print.

Would you believe that fossils from the sea can be found in a desert? It's true. They have even been discovered on top of mountains! They prove that the spot where they were found was once an ocean floor.

Scientists can tell us some interesting fossil facts. There are certain plants and animals that lived in hot climates. Their fossils have been found in cold countries. This proves that these areas were not always cold. Geologists study the rock layer in which the fossils were found. Then they can tell when the country was warm and for how long.

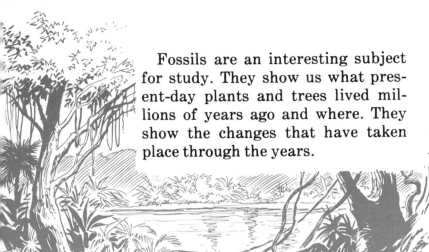

Fossils are an interesting subject for study. They show us what present-day plants and trees lived millions of years ago and where. They show the changes that have taken place through the years.

An unusual type of fossil is petrified wood or bone. A chemical known as silica replaced each cell of original matter. Slowly the material turned to stone. Today it looks just as it did millions of years ago.

You probably can find some fossils in your own neighborhood. Look in diggings, road cuts, or streambanks. Look wherever cuts have been made through layers of sedimentary rock.

If you don't know a good place to hunt for fossils, ask your teacher. Or, write to a college geology department in your state.

YOUR EQUIPMENT

- Geologist's hammer for pulling rocks out of the hillside and breaking them open.
- Cold chisel, ½ inch to 1 inch wide. It is for chipping stone with a hammer and for digging things loose.
- Small notebook and pencil for recording where and when you found a sample.
- Safety glasses for your protection.
- A pocket magnifier for seeing things up close.
- Newspapers for wrapping rocks you want to carry.
- A small day pack. It is used for carrying tools, rocks, newspapers, and heavy gloves for rough work.

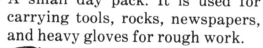

YOUR COLLECTION

Divide three trays or drawers into sections. Mark the drawers sedimentary, igneous, and metamorphic. This will separate your rocks and keep them from being scratched. Each sample should have a number. Every drawer or tray section should have a card. It should list number, name, date, and place found.

WHERE TO HUNT

Try to find a business that sells building stone or one that makes and sells gravestones. The phone book can help. You probably can get small stone scraps from them. You may get marble, granite, sandstone, limestone, pumice, shale, or slate.

Look in gravel or sand pits, road cuts, diggings, mountains, hills, and streambanks. Quarries and mine dump heaps are good, but they can be dangerous. Always have an adult with you. Be careful when climbing on rocks or cliffs. Stay away from old mines.

Watch out for snakes. They crawl under rocks to get out of the sun. Learn to poke around a rock with a stick before work—always!

Keep your rock samples small. Small ones are easier to carry and easier to care for.

Collecting samples is not allowed in the national parks.

GEOLOGIST
SCOREBOARD

Requirements

RDL
11-24-81
PDL
11-24-81

RDL
11-24-81
RDL
12/8/81

RDL
11-24-81

136

NATURALIST

Do you know what a naturalist is? You should, because you have been one all your life.

A naturalist is a person who studies plants or animals. You have watched your pets or other animals in your neighborhood. You have looked at grass, flowers, and shrubs in your yard. You wondered how they grew. That makes you a naturalist.

For this activity badge, you can go much further toward becoming a real naturalist. You could keep an "insect zoo." You can care for fish or small animals. You can learn things about the plants near your home. Perhaps you will visit a real zoo or take a hike in the woods. There you will see wild animals and forest plants.

All this will prepare you for the great adventure of nature study when you become a Scout.

The real naturalist has a pair of sharp eyes and a great love for nature. He sees things that other people miss. This is because he knows where to look and what his eyes show him. Whenever you are outdoors, watch for the flash of a squirrel's tail. Look for the little mound that leads to busy ants. Don't just dawdle along and scuff your shoes on a hike. Look and listen for nature's secrets. Know what they are!

COMPLETE FOUR OF THE FOLLOWING:

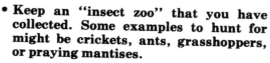

- **Keep an "insect zoo" that you have collected. Some examples to hunt for might be crickets, ants, grasshoppers, or praying mantises.**

- **Set up an aquarium or terrarium. Keep it for a month. Use plants and animals you have collected.**

- **Visit a museum of natural history, nature center, or zoo with family, den, or pack. Tell what you saw.**

- **Read a nature book on birds, insects, fish, snakes, or other wild animals. Or, read about plants or the life of a naturalist.**

- **Make a chart showing the flyways used by North American birds.**

- **Be able to identify the poisonous plants and reptiles found in your area.**

- **Watch six wild animals (snakes, turtles, fish, birds, or mammals) in the wild. Describe the kind of place (forest, field, marsh, yard, or park) where you saw them. Tell what they were doing.**

INSECTS

All things in nature are interrelated. Insects are eaten by frogs. Frogs are eaten by fishes. Fishes are caught by larger animals, including man.

Many natural forces control the number of insects. Some are spiders and other animal-eating invertebrates (backboneless creatures). Others include fishes, amphibians, reptiles, birds, animals, disease, parasites, weather, and accidents. Predation (eating another animal) and parasitism (living on another animal) by other insects are important. Some wasps make nests, find caterpillars, and sting them. Each wasp places the paralyzed caterpillar in its nest. It lays an egg on the caterpillar and seals the entrance. When the egg hatches, it feeds on the caterpillar.

The real fun comes in watching butterflies and moths go through their different stages of life: egg, larva, pupa, and adult.

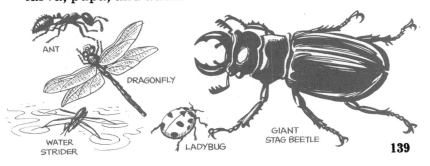

ANT

DRAGONFLY

WATER STRIDER

LADYBUG

GIANT STAG BEETLE

You may find the cocoon or chrysalis (pupa stage). You can watch the insect come out as a moth or butterfly.

EGGS **1**

2 CATERPILLAR (LARVA)

3
PUPA
(CHRYSALIS)

You can find egg masses, cocoons, and chrysalises almost anywhere. Look on the trees and shrubs near home or on trees and bushes in the park. Look in tool sheds and garages. Hunt under rocks.

4
MORNING CLOAK

Whatever you find, treat it gently. Carry it home in a shoebox. If it is on a branch, cut off enough to make it easy to handle. About 6 to 8 inches should do. In your notebook, write where and when you found it. Note the place where you found it.

YOUR ZOO

Build the cages to fit the insect. Here are a few ideas:

PRAYING MANTIS

Use a round tin can with plastic lid. Have a 12-inch piece of screen long enough to go around the can. Have an inch for overlap. Make tube from screening. Lace together with wire.

Set wire tube in can. Fill bottom of can with plaster of paris. Push branch with egg mass into plaster of paris before it hardens. Put cover of can on top of screen tube.

Food: flies, small insects, tiny bits of raw liver, chopped meat. The mantis prefers live food.

Water: Put in bottle cap.

BUTTERFLIES AND MOTHS

A widemouth jar with a screw top makes a good zoo. Punch air holes in the top. Put in the branch of the plant or tree on which you found the caterpillar. Keep a fresh supply of the same leaves in the jar until it stops eating. Then it enters the cocoon or chrysalis stage. It will become a moth or butterfly.

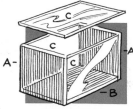

MATERIALS
A – WOOD ¾"× 5¾"× 6"
B – WOOD ¾"× 5¾"× 8"
C – GLASS 6"× 9½"

FIELD CRICKETS

Put a toothpick under glass to give cricket air. Sink bottle-cap drinking fountains in soil.

Use catsup or pop-bottle caps. Place 2 inches of soil in bottom of cage.

Food: water-soaked bread, mashed potatoes, lettuce, peanut butter.

Keep bottle caps full of water.

YOUR ANT HOUSE

Make U-frame of scraps of wood 1 by 1 by 10 inches. Fasten in center of wood base 1 by 6 by 12 inches. Glue and tape two pieces of glass 10 by 11 inches to the wood strips.

Dig up anthill and put in the house. Tape top on after ants are in. Put a sponge in place. Stuff the air holes with cotton. Soak the sponge with water once a week. Keep soil moist, but not wet.

Food: small bits of sugar, peanuts, apples, bananas every few days.

Keep the house covered when not watching it. Ants like to work in the dark.

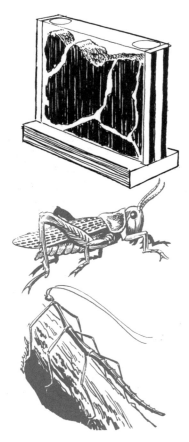

GRASSHOPPERS— WALKING STICKS

Cover bottom of jar with an inch of soil. Cover this with grass sod. Water grass occasionally. Punch air holes in the cover. Put a water dish in the jar.

Food: water and grass.

CLICK BEETLES

Keep a dish of water in the jar. Feed them flies, mealworms, and other soft-bodied insects.

Keep your cages in a shady spot.

KNOWING INSECTS

In the woods there are dangerous plants and animals. You should know these.

To keep cocoons, chrysalises, or egg masses during winter, ask your parents to leave on a window screen. Place the twigs inside the screen but outside the window. Keep the window closed all the time. Then nature will take care of things. Best of all, your butterflies or moths will come out at the right time.

It's a good idea to check the cocoons and chrysalises when you gather them. If there are small holes in them, chances are they are empty. If they rattle when you shake them gently, probably the pupa is dead.

You won't have time to study every insect while you are a Webelos Scout. Still, there are doors that you can open for yourself. You can learn which insects are harmful to man and which are helpful. Spend some time outdoors watching insects at work. Learn to tell the good guys from the bad!

Insects aren't all bad. They help to give us food and flowers by pollination. They improve the soil. They eat harmful insects or their eggs or larvae.

HELPFUL INSECTS

Among the helpful insects are the predators. (Remember—They eat other insects.) They are—

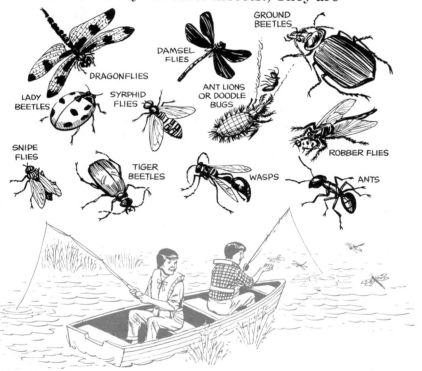

DRAGONFLIES: Three hundred kinds of the 2,000 known ones live in the United States. You can find them along ponds, lakes, swamps, and slow-moving streams. Maybe you have seen these brightly colored, dainty-winged insects. Perhaps you know them as darning needles or mosquito hawks.

They can see in all directions at once because of the curve of their eyes. These have as many as 20,000 windows. Two pairs of wings give them great speed.

While flying, they scoop mosquitos, their only food, out of the air. They form a sort of basket with their legs. Moving their jaws sideways, they eat their catch while still flying.

The young are called nymphs. They live on the bottom of streams and ponds among the rocks. They feed on mosquitoes and other insects in the water. The time it takes them to grow to full size (1 to 2 inches) varies. It can be several months to 3 or 4 years.

At this stage, the nymph crawls out onto a reed, root, or rock. When it has dried off, the skin splits down the back. The dragonfly pulls itself out of its skin. It then spreads its wings to dry. The beautiful colors appear. Soon the big mosquito hunt begins.

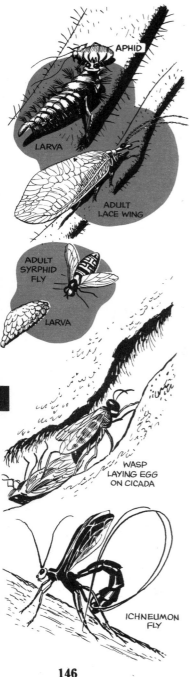

APHID-LIONS: This group includes the dobsonflies, ant lions, and the golden-eyed lacewings. They are among the most helpful insects of prey. They destroy the eggs of many harmful caterpillars. They eat all stages of plant-feeding mites, scale insects, aphids, and mealy bugs.

CARNIVORES

LADY BEETLES (BUGS): These insects destroy the eggs and young of aphids, scales, and other soft-bodied, plant-eating insects.

HERBIVORE: PLANT-EATING

SYRPHID FLIES: This fly is helpful in crop pollination. It destroys plant pests, especially aphids.

PARASITIC INSECTS (PARASITES)

This is a very interesting and useful group. These insects attack all kinds of other insects. They destroy them by laying eggs or putting their young on insect, egg, or larva.

The young feed on the host until nearly full grown.

The two-winged flies and the wasps are the most important of this group. Because of their great numbers, they are the ones most often seen.

146

LAYING EGGS
ON CATERPILLAR

TACHINID FLIES: These flies kill many common insects, especially caterpillars.

THE FLESH FLIES: They feed on grasshoppers (grasshopper maggot).

YELLOW JACKET: This one feeds on corn, earworm, armyworm, and Polistes.

MUD DAUBER: This insect kills soft-bodied insects and spiders.

HORSE GUARDS: They feed on horseflies, horn flies, and stable flies.

Insects are tireless pollinizers. Usually we think only of butterflies and bees when we think of pollinization. We should remember that ants, beetles, flies, and wasps do it too.

YELLOW JACKET

MUD DAUBER

POISONOUS REPTILES

GILA MONSTER: This animal grows to about 2 feet long. The lighter part of the pattern is white or yellow. It is found in Arizona and Nevada.

CORAL SNAKE: This snake grows to be about 3 feet long. It is ringed with red, black, and yellow bands. It is found from Kentucky and North Carolina south to Florida and Texas.

GILA MONSTER

CORAL SNAKE

147

EASTERN DIAMONDBACK RATTLESNAKE: This one sometimes grows to 7 feet in length. It is found along the Atlantic coast from North Carolina to Florida and west to Louisiana. It is never more than 100 miles from the coast.

WESTERN DIAMONDBACK RATTLESNAKE: It often grows to 7 feet in length. It lives in the southwestern United States. The area is from Missouri and eastern Texas to southeastern California.

TIMBER RATTLESNAKE: This snake is under 6 feet in length. It is found in much of the eastern United States. It is not seen in the midwest except in a strip from southern Wisconsin to Texas.

SIDEWINDER OR HORNED RATTLESNAKE: It is found in the deserts of the Southwest.

PRAIRIE RATTLESNAKE: It is about 3 feet in length. Sometimes it grows to 5 feet. It lives in the western half of the United States.

WATER MOCCASIN (cottonmouth): This snake is found in or near water from southeastern Virginia to Florida. It can be seen westward to east Texas and north as far as southwestern Illinois. It sometimes grows as long as 6 feet.

COPPERHEAD: Not often longer than 4 feet, it lives in most all southeastern states. It can be found as far north as Massachusetts, Pennsylvania, and the Midwest. It has been seen in Colorado.

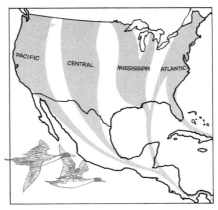

MIGRATION OF BIRDS

Do you know what migration means? It is movement from one place to another. This can be of birds, animals, and even people. You may have seen flocks of birds flying over your area toward another. This is migration.

Ornithologists (scientists who study birds) don't know exactly why birds migrate. Many birds move as winter draws near. Cold weather and snow make it hard for them to find food. Yet some birds leave long before cold weather sets in. There's lots of food, yet they fly away. So we can't be certain just why these migrate.

We do know what routes the birds take. In spring and fall, the birds travel up and down main routes. These are called flyways. The map shows the most heavily used ones in the United States.

You don't have to live on a flyway to see birds moving in the spring and fall. Some will pass over your town. But, most flocks use the flyways. They are their highways between winter and summer homes.

149

NATURALIST SCOREBOARD
Requirements

Approved by

DO FOUR:

RPL
6J 2/17/82

- Keep an "insect zoo" that you have collected. Some examples to hunt for might be crickets, ants, grasshoppers, or praying mantises.   141

- Set up an aquarium or terrarium. Keep it for a month. Use plants and animals you have collected.   141

RPL
6J 2/17/82

- Visit a museum of natural history, nature center, or zoo with your family, den, or pack. Tell what you saw.

RPL
6J 2/17/82

- Read a nature book on birds, insects, fish, snakes, or other wild animals. Or, read about plants or the life of a naturalist.

- Make a chart showing the flyways used by North American birds.   149

- Be able to identify the poisonous plants and reptiles found in your area.   147, 176

RPL
6J 2/17/82

- Watch six wild animals (snakes, turtles, fish, birds, or mammals) in the wild. Describe the kind of place (forest, field, marsh, yard, or park) where you saw them. Tell what they were doing.

OUTDOORSMAN

You are a step closer to your goal of being a Scout now. As a Webelos Scout, you will do some outdoor things. They will help to prepare you for Scouting.

Of course, you won't camp out with others for days as Scouts do. That will have to wait until you are a Scout.

But you can learn some things you will need to know as a camper. To earn the Outdoorsman badge, you may camp out with your own family. You can learn to cook outdoors. You can make and sleep in a tent in your own or a friend's backyard.

Have fun. Learn all the outdoor things you can so you will be ready.

COMPLETE FIVE
OF THE FOLLOWING PROJECTS
TO DEMONSTRATE YOUR SKILL:

- Make a backyard tent. Sleep in it 4 nights. Camp in your own or your friend's backyard.

- Help with a camp-out 5 nights away from home with your family. (It doesn't need to be all at one time.)

- With your family or den, plan and take part in an evening outdoor activity which has a campfire.

- Help cook your own lunch or supper outdoors with your parents or another grown-up. Clean up afterward.

- Know and practice the rules of outdoor fire safety.

- Take part in one of your den's outdoor activities.

- Visit your Scout camp with your den.

THE GREAT OUTDOORS

Camping is knowing how to live comfortably outdoors. If you live in a house, the outdoors begins just outside your back door. In an apartment, you may have to walk to the front or back door. But the outdoors is still there waiting for you.

You can do your camping in your own backyard if you have one. You can camp in a friend's backyard or a little-used corner of the apartment yard. Always ask permission before you put your camp on someone else's land. You could even ask your own parents for a place.

You can learn how to camp by backyard camping. Most good campers try things out close to home first. Scouts begin that way. You can learn to put up your own tent. You can make a comfortable bed on the ground. You can build a safe fire, cook your meals, and clean up afterward.

REMEMBER THIS.

The cleaner the area

The safer the fire

The better the meals

The drier the tent

The better the bed

The happier the
outdoorsman!

Backyard camping is more fun when you are doing it with your best friend. Prepare for it just as though you were going to be miles away from home. Plan what you'll need to sleep in and the clothes you'll wear. Plan your food. How about water? Think about your tent and the tools you'll need. Once you've hiked out the back door to your campsite, stay there. Stay until the camping trip is over. Don't run back and forth to the house except for a great emergency.

YOUR TENT

One of the first things that you plan is your tent. You want one that's light. It should keep you dry in wet weather and cool in hot weather. A good one is made from a square. It's just a big piece of material. It has grommets (brass eyes) or tapes set in along all four sides. With the help of a grown-up, make one. Use this pattern.

You'll need 11¾ yards of 43-inch material. Cut three pieces 10 feet 9 inches long. Sew them together into one large sheet. Hem all edges.

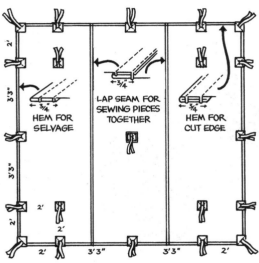

LAP SEAM FOR SEWING PIECES TOGETHER

HEM FOR SELVAGE

HEM FOR CUT EDGE

CENTER TAPES   TAPES ALONG HEMS   CORNER TAPES

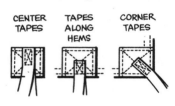

Make twenty-one 2-inch-wide by 21½-inch-long strips for tying tapes. Make them from eleven 2-inch strips of material, full width. Fold edges back ¼ inch. Fold in half lengthwise. Sew the edges.

Make twenty-six 4-inch squares for reinforcement patches. Cut from three 4-inch strips of material, full width. Fold edges under ¼ inch. Sew on big square as shown. Extra patch goes on underside of tarp. Sew tying tapes onto patches.

You can use many kinds of cloth, from old flour sacks to balloon cloth. Good unbleached muslin makes a good tent from cheap material. Even a bed sheet will work. It will make a smaller tent, however. You may dye or decorate a tent before waterproofing it.

You can buy a cheap, nonflammable waterproofing mixture from mail order houses. Spread your tent upon the grass or a flat surface to dry after waterproofing.

You can use this tent in many ways. It can be used as a ground cloth or a cover for your gear. You can put it up in different ways too. One way is over a rope or clothes wire. Tie the rope or wire between two trees or buildings or posts. Stretch the tent out and peg down the sides. To make a lean-to, fasten one end to a fence, building, pole, or clothesline. Peg the other end to the ground.

PITCH HIGH AND DRY

Put your tent on a level spot—one that's high and dry. You'll be all wet if you wake up with your bed in water. Pitch your tent so the early morning sun shines in it.

YOUR BEDDING

For a good bed, go over the ground. Get down on your hands and knees. Carefully feel all around. Pick up any sticks and stones. A small stone can feel like a big rock before morning. Make a light canvas bag, bed size. Fill it with dry grass, hay, or straw. This works like a mattress. Well—almost!

Put a ground cloth under your bed. It will keep out the cold and damp of the earth. This can be an old shower curtain, raincoat, or waterproof cloth.

Make an envelope bed as shown:

1. **Lay the first blanket on the ground. Put the second blanket half on and half off the first one.**

2. **Fold the first blanket over the second. Leave half of the second showing.**

3. **Fold the remaining half of the second blanket back over the first. This gives you two thicknesses over you and under you.**

4. **Fold the bottom of the blankets up.**

5. **Fasten the blanket envelope with big blanket pins up both sides and on bottom.**

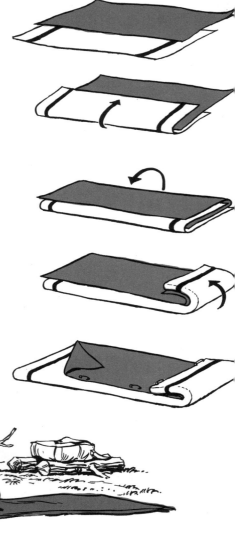

FAMILY CAMPING

Project 2 for the Outdoorsman asks you to help with a family camp-out. This is for 5 nights away from home. They do not have to be in a row. The word to remember is "help."

You expect to have your share of the fun on a family camp-out, of course. But as an outdoorsman, you will also want to help with the planning and work.

Here are some things you need to know to make your family's camp-out safe and fun. You can do this by telling them these things:

SNAKES: They are not likely to bother you if you don't bother them. Stay away from them.

INSECTS: A good bug spray keeps most of them away.

POISON PLANTS: Know poison ivy, poison oak, and poison sumac and stay away from them. Never eat anything from the woods unless you know exactly what it is.

ANIMALS: They are drawn to your camp by the food that you throw away or leave out. Mice, chipmunks, raccoons, opossums, porcupines, and skunks add to the adventure of camping out. Watch them and enjoy them. DON'T try to catch or pet them. Bears are the most dangerous camp raiders or roadside beggars. YOU must remember that THEY are NOT tame. Never let your little brothers or sisters get near them.

SWIMMING: Always swim with a grown-up. Watch for drop-offs or holes and bad currents. Don't swim in polluted water! Don't get too much sun or get tired.

CLEANLINESS: On a family camping trip you want to rough it. Be as rough as you like, but don't be dirty. Greasy dishes, bad water, and spoiled food can ruin your trip. Wash dishes in warm water and dip in boiling water. Use pliers to dunk metal dishes. Air-dry your dishes on a plastic sheet.

GETTING LOST: It can happen to anyone, even mothers and fathers. Make keeping your brothers and sisters safe your job. Give them whistles for their pockets or to wear around their necks. Be sure that you have YOURS. If you get lost, sit down. Relax. Blow your whistle every so often. Stay put.

160

FOR THE CAR

You should make a list of things you might forget. Things you will want to have handy in the car include:

☐	sunglasses	insect spray	☐
☐	extra eyeglasses (or lens prescription)	suntan lotion	☐
☐	car pillow	canteen	☐
☐	blanket	desert water bag	☐
☐	tote-litter bag	swim trunks	☐
☐	road maps of the area	tennis or beach shoes	☐
☐	whistle	raincoat or poncho	☐
☐	pocketknife	boots or galoshes	☐
☐	camera	umbrella	☐
☐	flashlight or lantern	car games	☐

Talk this over with mother or dad. Be sure they are planning on a munchin' bag for snacks.

LOADING AND UNLOADING

One of the things you can do is to help load and unload the car. Pack things in the order they will be used.

Everything has its place. Clothing should be to the back, with stove and cooking equipment to one side. Sleeping gear should be on the other side and tent and poles on top. The tents come out first to make camp.

Here are some packing hints:
- Keep packages small.
- Use canvas bags, plastic cases, or small boxes. Different colored tags for each person make it easier to find that person's things.
- Pack things in the order that you will be using them.

HANDY SACK FOR THE CAR

You need a handy sack for the car too. Here is another thing you can do to help: Get these things together and put them in a small box or plastic bag. Check them off as you pack.

☐ paper napkins
☐ tissues
☐ dust cloth
☐ damp sponge or washcloths in plastic bags for car cleanup
☐ whisk broom or brush

☐ bottle opener
☐ can opener
☐ paper cups
☐ drinking straws
☐ road maps for the area
☐ plastic bags to hold swimsuits or wet clothing

☐ first aid kit
☐ fly swatter
☐ roll of paper towels to wipe off windshield

162

PACK YOUR OWN THINGS

Here is a list of things for your family. Roll and pack the clothes; they'll be less wrinkled. Put things that might break inside small plastic bags. Then roll them all up inside your robe or pajamas.

pajamas

slippers

bathrobes

shower cap

change of underwear

extra socks, stockings

plastic bags for
damp clothes

sewing kit

clean shirt,
blouse, or sweater

toothbrushes

toothpaste

shaving gear

cosmetics

manicuring set

brushes and combs

face soap

detergent (for laundry)

safety pins

ON THE TRIP

On the family trip to camp, you can help your parents. "Baby-sit" with younger brothers and sisters if you have any. Try to make the trip fun for everyone. Do this by obeying these simple rules: Stay in your seat. Leave door handles alone. Keep doors locked. Keep your arms, head, or toys out of the car windows. Large toys, such as balloons or swimming rings, should be kept packed. Pencils or other sharp things are not toys. (A sudden stop might throw you forward and they could stab someone.) Use your litter bag for paper and trash. Leave the controls of the car alone. Don't fight.

BABY-SITTING ✳✳✳✳✳✳✳✳✳✳✳✳✳✳✳✳✳✳✳✳✳

If your mother asks you to care for the younger children, try playing these games:

ROAD SIGN ALPHABET ✳✳✳✳✳✳✳✳✳✳✳✳✳✳✳✳✳

If there are just two children, try this game. One watches the left side of the road. The other watches the right. A child seeing the letter *A* on a sign on his side calls out *A*. Then he looks for *B*, and each letter in turn. He can use only one letter from each sign that he sees. The first going from A to Z wins.

WHO AM I? ✳✳✳✳✳✳✳✳✳✳✳✳✳✳✳✳✳✳✳✳✳✳✳✳✳✳✳

One child is "It." The others get together and give him a new identity. That is, they make believe that he is someone or something else. They don't tell him who he's supposed to be. "It" must ask questions. He may ask "Am I a person?" or "Am I an animal?" Or he might ask "Am I in a story?" The other players answer "Yes" or "No" or "I don't know." "It" has a certain length of time to find out who he is.

CONTINUED STORY ✳✳✳✳✳✳✳✳✳✳✳✳✳✳✳✳✳

This can be lots of fun for everybody, even your mother and father. Somebody starts telling a story. It may be a story that he has read. It may be one that he makes up as he goes along. Suddenly he quits. The next player picks up the story and adds to it. Then he stops. The next person begins. The last player has to end it. There are no winners—just fun.

CRAYON AND PAPER GAMES ★★★★★★★★★★★★

Don't use pencils in the car. They are too sharp. If the driver must stop suddenly, a person holding a pencil might jab somebody. Crayons are OK because they are not sharp.

TICKTACKTOE ★★★★★★★★★★★★★★★★★★★★★★★★★★★

Here's an old one you probably know. Even younger children can play it with you once they get the idea.

DOODLING ★★★★★★★★★★★★★★★★★★★★★★★★★★★★★

Have each child write his initials on a sheet of paper. If he can't write, do it for him. Then tell him to draw a picture. Have him use the lines of his initials as the start.

HOW TO GET THERE ★★★★★★★★★★★★★★★★★★★★

Borrow an old road map. Give each child two cities on the map. If he can't read, draw circles around the cities for him. Then ask each one to get from one city to the other. Have him trace the different roads he can use. Each child should have a different colored crayon to use.

FIRE BUILDING

Preparing and cooking your own meals outdoors is lots of fun. How good you feel, dishing up fine food that you have cooked over a campfire! It smells good—it even tastes better.

A good outdoor cook knows certain things. He can build a fire and control it. He knows that wind can spread sparks. He knows that fire can creep through dry grass, leaves, or pine needles. He knows that some rocks burst when heated. He knows that spilled bacon grease can spread fire or cause bad burns.

Your den chief can be a great help to you in learning outdoor cooking. Always have him or an adult around just in case of emergency.

The best place to learn outdoor cooking is in your mother's kitchen, with her help. She can teach you to fry, boil, broil, bake, and roast. She'll show you how to clean up. Once you can do these, you can move outdoors.

OUTDOOR FIRESAFETY RULES

1. Almost every campsite or picnic area has its rules. Learn them and obey them.

2. Clear a circle 4 to 6 feet across of everything that will burn.

3. Set up your stove or build your fire in the center. There will be less chance of your fire getting away.

4. Don't build your fire against a tree or between the roots.

5. Keep your fire away from dead logs or stumps.

6. Don't use firewood that spits sparks.

7. Break your burnt matches before you throw them away.

8. Never leave your fire alone.

9. Keep a bucket of water or sand handy for emergency use.

10. When you are through with your fire, put it out. Spread the coals and ashes and sprinkle them with water. Stir and sprinkle until the fire is cold out. This means it feels cold to your hand.

An outdoorsman cooks over coals on a small fire.

If you have a charcoal grill in your backyard, use it. Or you may want to make your own stove out of a No. 10 tin can. A stove uses less fuel. It gives you a hotter, well-controlled fire. The drawings show two ways to make a stove.

You can make a good fireplace out of rocks. Shale and sandstone burst. Don't use them.

OUTDOOR COOKERY

Start out with something easy to prepare—a hike lunch. Include the things you like best. As you plan it, think about meat, bread, drink, fruit, vegetables, and sweets.

For this kind of meal, cold sliced meats or dried chipped beef are easiest. When you have your first cookout, try hamburgers, bacon, eggs, or hot dogs. Later, try fish, steak, or chicken.

VEGETABLES	LIQUIDS	FRUIT
Carrots	Milk	Raisins
Tomatoes	Canteen of water	Dried fruit
Radishes	Orange	Apples
Onions	Ripe tomato	Oranges
Pickles	BREAD	Dates
Celery	The kind you like	OTHER
		Hard-boiled egg—salt
		Cheese
SWEETS	CRACKERS	Cream cheese—jelly
Chocolate bars	Rye crisp	Peanut butter—jelly
Marshmallows	Graham	Fruit cookies
Fruit tablets	Soda or fancy	Nuts

Don't use foods that are sticky or soft. Pack your lunch carefully. Wrap paper towels around things that might be crushed. Stand sandwiches on end. The bread stays tastier that way.

When it's warm out, carry your milk in a Thermos bottle. You might use a canteen of water instead. Be smart—leave soda at home. It's heavy to carry and hard to keep cool. There's little food value in it.

Many good meals can be prepared outdoors without using pots and pans. Try aluminum foil to wrap vegetables and ground beef. Put the package right on the coals. Let it cook for about a half hour.

A RHYME OF FIREWOODS

Oak and ash and birch
and beech,
Larch and spruce and pine,
All will make a fire good,
All will brightly shine.
Ash and oak are hard
and slow,
Birch and beech are gay,
Larch, spruce, pine will
start your flame
In the woodsman's way.
Elder, elm, and poplar
boughs
Smoky fuel seem,
Willow wood is never used
By a camper keen.
Oak or ash or birch
or beech,
Larch or spruce or pine,
Take your pick, but ash
is best,
Green or dry, 'tis fine.

OAK

ASH

BIRCH

BEECH

LARCH

SPRUCE

ALDER

POPLAR

PINE

ELM

WILLOW

171

HOW TO USE SAFETY CAN OPENER

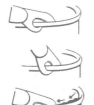

- Fit short hook under outside lip of can.
- Lift handle—edge cuts down into can along inside.
- Lower handle—move toward you and cut again.
- Cut all around—do it slowly until you learn how.

CUTTING BLADE CAN OPENER LEATHER PUNCH CAP LIFTER SCREW DRIVER

SMALL BLADE

AN OUTDOORSMAN'S TOOL KIT

Your pocketknife is a fine tool kit. It has a cutting blade, can opener, leather punch, cap lifter, and screwdriver.

For an outdoor activity, backyard camp, or family camping trip, you need very few tools. They are your dish, cup, knife, fork, spoon, and pocketknife (tool kit).

HOW TO USE YOUR KNIFE

- Cut away from yourself—always.
- Close your blade carefully. With one hand, hold handle tightly. Close with palm of other.
- Handle it with care so that you don't cut yourself or anyone else.
- Use it only on things that won't dull or break the blade. Keep if off the ground.

OUTDOOR ACTIVITIES

Your den's outdoor activities may have nature hikes or rock hunts. There may be hikes down adventure trails or walks to good fishing spots. Knowing how to get there safely and comfortably will add to the fun.

With your den, practice these simple hike rules. Prepare yourself for the big outdoor adventures of Scouting.

A good rule is never go alone. Go with your den leader and den chief. Start with a short hike. Take it easy. Really see the things that you pass. Look at the trees. Try to name as many kinds as you can. Look at the houses and barns. Count the different kinds of birds that you see.

When you sit down for a rest, look around. Find grasses that are not the same. Count the different bugs that you find. Outdoor activities are much more fun that way. Some people go as if they were walking through a tunnel. They never see a thing.

For your first hike, choose a place about a mile or so from your town. It may be a park, a high hill, a pond, or a lake. Perhaps there's a grove of trees or a picnic area nearby. Out and back would be a 2- or 3-mile trip—a pretty good start. Set your own pace. Hike for 15 minutes. Rest for 5 minutes. Then try a 20-minute walk and a 10-minute rest. Stay together. Try different speeds until you find one best for all.

Walk a little every week. Go farther each time. This makes you stronger.

Face traffic when walking along a road. This means walk on the left side. Walk single file when the whole den goes. If you walk at night, carry a light or wear white.

Watch for signs and landmarks so you can find your way back.

WHAT TO WEAR

The Webelos Scout uniform is ideal for hiking. Take along a raincoat and an extra pair of socks.

SHOES: You depend upon your shoes to get you there and back. Choose them carefully. Take good care of them. A high-top shoe is best because it keeps out gravel and sand. You may not have a pair. If not, roll your socks over the tops of your low shoes. The roll will keep the sand and gravel out.

It's very important that your hiking shoes fit well. If they don't, you'll be sure to get blisters. The shoes should be fairly tight around your heel. There should be room to wiggle your toes.

- Never go hiking in new shoes. Break them in first by wearing them every day for a week or more.
- To keep your shoes soft and partly waterproof, rub them with saddle soap. Do this before and after every hike.
- When leather shoes get wet, wipe them out with paper or old socks. Dry them slowly away from direct heat.

SOCKS: Socks are almost as important as shoes. Wool socks soak up moisture. They also let air get to your skin and cushion your feet. Take an extra pair on a hike. Then you can wash your feet and put on clean socks before you start back. This dry pair will feel great. Don't use socks with holes or holes that have been darned. They start blisters.

Camping or resting near a hornets' or wasps' nest is inviting trouble. Do not disturb. Their stings can be bad news.

OUTDOORSMAN SCOREBOARD

SCHOLAR

You may think that your schoolwork is hard and dull. But where else can you learn the "what" and the "why" of so many things? You learn to read and write and work with numbers. You find out what other countries and people are like. These all can make your life much more interesting.

To earn this badge, you must do several things that you probably are doing already. These are going to school every day, earning the best grades you can, and behaving well.

COMPLETE THESE FOUR REQUIREMENTS

- Have a good record in attendance, behavior, and grades at school.

- Take an active part in a school activity or service.

- Discuss with your teacher or principal the value of having an education.

- List in writing some important things you can do now because of going to school.

AND DO ANY THREE OF THE FOLLOWING:

- Trace back through history the different kinds of schools. Tell how our present public school system grew out of these early schools.

- Make a chart showing how your school system is run.

- Ask your parents and five other grown-ups these questions:

  a. What do you think are the best things about my school?

  b. What are its main problems?

  What do you think were the best answers? Why?

- List and explain some of the full-time positions in the education field.

- Help another student with his school-work. Tell what you did to help.

What do you do every day? You sleep and eat. You go to school and eat, and you come home and eat. Then you play and eat again. But how much time do you spend doing this?

You have 24 hours every day, just as everyone else does. What do you do with them? Fill in the times below as closely as you can:

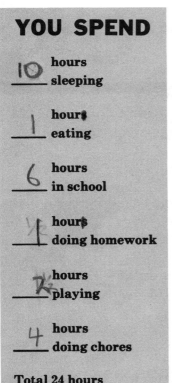

YOU SPEND

10 hours
sleeping

1 hours
eating

6 hours
in school

1 hours
doing homework

2 hours
playing

4 hours
doing chores

Total 24 hours

Each day can be a new adventure filled with happy activities. You can learn new games or master new skills. Or a day can be dull, uninteresting, and dreary.

Add them up—6 or more hours each day are spent in school. So, isn't it smart for you to try to enjoy those hours as much as you can?

What is a school anyway? It could be just a building—like jail—where you are kept against your will. Or it could be a happy place where you meet your friends every day. It could make your life more interesting because it's where you find out new things. You learn to read and write and to use and understand the meaning of figures.

School is a lot more fun when you take part in all the things going on. Maybe you can't play on the team or help with some of the projects. Don't let that stop you. Be a good booster—you can help build school spirit that way.

Do you really want to find out what school means to you? List all the things that you can do now but couldn't do before you attended school. You can:

1. Read
2. Write
3. Do arithmetic
4. Sing new songs
5. Tell the history of your state and your country
6. Know geography
   List others.

If your school has special things to do outside the classroom, try to take part. Maybe you can do a service job. Ask your teacher.

Here are some things you might try doing to pass the second requirement:

• Play in the school band.
• Be in the safety patrol.
• Be a library helper.

When you are grown up, you'll find this out: The more you know, the better your life will be.

There is another important value of school. If you are educated, you can take your place as a fine citizen. You will have the knowledge and the understanding to do this. Talk with your teacher about this.

180

HISTORY OF SCHOOLS

Your school is the latest step on a long trail going back to the cavemen. Long before men learned to read and write, there were "schools." The "teachers" were mothers and fathers. The "subjects" were hunting, fishing, cooking, and child care.

In the earliest written records of ancient men, there are stories of schools. These schools were in the temples, where the people worshiped their gods. Mostly they taught things about religion.

Perhaps the most advanced of the ancient men were Egyptians. In Egypt, the temple schools taught more and more subjects as the years went on.

Four hundred years before Christ, the Greeks and the Romans were the most advanced people. Both believed that schools were important. Both had teachers.

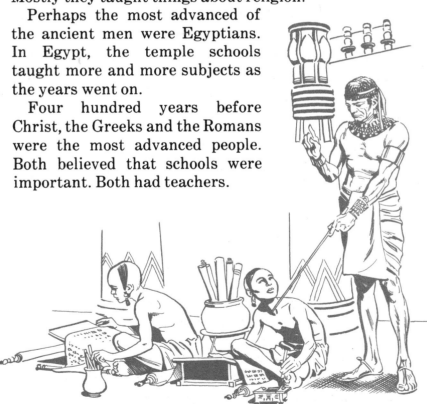

Their schools were not like ours. Sometimes the teacher just walked around the streets with his pupils and talked to them. Or he might meet them in a garden or the woods. A great Greek teacher named Plato met his students in a garden in Athens called the Academy. That's where the word "academy," meaning school, came from. Only in the last hundred years has school been important to most people. Before that, just the richest persons went to school. Even today, our nation is unusual when it comes to education. We are one of the few countries with free schooling for all through high school.

America's colonists soon set up schools. The Pilgrims landed in 1620. By 1647 Massachusetts Colony had a law providing for free public schools. Few were set up, though. Most schools were still private.

New England had schools in homes, where children learned Bible verses and their ABCs. Academies trained boys for college. The Middle Colonies had both public and church-run private schools. In the Southern Colonies, each plantation had its own teacher.

It was not until the 1800's that free schools were found in most places. People did not think that the public schools were very good. If they could afford to, parents still sent their children to private academies. The main subjects were the "Three R's"—Readin', 'Ritin', and 'Rithmetic.

These schools were not much like yours. Usually there was just one room. Boys sat on one side and girls on the other. Sometimes children—especially those from farms—came only when there was no work at home. Often everyone studied aloud at one time in the classroom! This was called a "Blab School."

The public schools we have today grew out of that kind of school.

People build and set up schools to help you improve your abilities. You should try to be on time. You should have a good attendance record. Your father and mother attend to their jobs. Also, the more interest you show in your lessons, the better your grades should be.

Of course, no one expects you to be either an angel or a superman! Just try your hardest each time that you do something. Then you should find that your best keeps getting better.

THE COST OF SCHOOLS

Public schools belong to the people. This means they are yours, your parents', and your neighbors'. So you, the people, must pay for them with taxes. If you attend a church-owned school, your parents and your church share the costs.

Schools cost money. Think of what they need. First, there must be classrooms and teachers for you. There must be principals and superintendents to run them and workers to clean them. There must be nurses and bus drivers. Last, there must be school boards. Your parents pay for all this with their school tax.

WHO RUNS YOUR SCHOOL?

The second requirement of the second part asks you to make a chart. It should show how your school system is run. The chart below is for a small city. It is just to give you an idea. Talk to your principal. Find out if your school system is like this. Then make up your own chart.

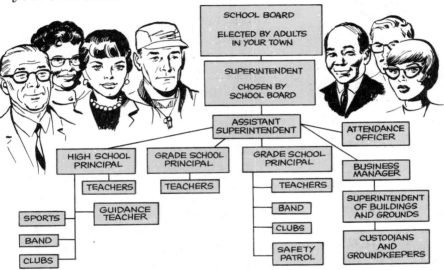

For the third requirement, ask your parents and five other adults about your school.

What do you think are the best things about your school? Is it good because of the subjects taught? Is the science course covered carefully, beginning with the kindergarten classes? Is the physical fitness program a good one? Are there good teachers? Is the school well located?

What are the school problems? What do you think could be done to solve them?

If you were going to improve something, what would you do to make it better? Whether it's an airplane, a house, or your school, you would look for its problems. You would find the things you don't like or the ones you think are weak. After listing the weak spots, you would look for what makes them that way. Then you would strengthen, improve, or replace the weak things.

You'll find out a lot about your school by talking with your parents and neighbors. Ask them what they think are the good things about your school system. Talk to them about its problems.

Do you know what full-time jobs are open to men in your school system? There are jobs in teaching, administration, and special services. Ask your teacher about other jobs for men in education.

Almost everything that you do can be more fun when shared with a friend. Games are more fun when played with others.

Helping a friend with his schoolwork is the same. It's showing him a thing or two that you have learned. It's more fun when you share what you know.

SCHOLAR SCOREBOARD
Requirements

Approved
by

DO ALL OF THESE:
- Have a good record in attendance, behavior, and grades at school.
- Take an active part in a school activity or service.   180
- Discuss with your teacher or principal the value of an education.   180
- List in writing some important things you can do now because of going to school.   180

AND DO THREE OF THESE:
- Trace back through history the different kinds of schools. Tell how our present public school system grew out of these early schools.   181
- Make a chart showing how your school system is run.   185
- Ask your parents and five other grown-ups these questions:
  a. What do you think are the best things about my school?
  b. What are its main problems?
  What do you think were the best answers? Why?
- List and explain some of the full-time positions open to men in the educational field.   187
- Help another student with his schoolwork. Tell what you did.   187

SCIENTIST

A scientist is a person who studies things to learn how they behave and why. He tries to find out the laws of nature about the things that he studies. People can use these rules or laws in making things. They know what the things that they are using will do.

Two other activity badge areas—Geologist and Naturalist—are scientific. In this one—Scientist—you will learn a few of the main ideas in physics. Physics is a science with several branches. One of these deals with weather. You can learn a little about weather in these activity badge requirements. One of these calls for learning what causes fog.

Another branch of physics is called optics. You will have a chance to work on this by learning something about light. You will find out how your eyes work.

Note that word "experiment." That is the key to the things for this activity badge. Scientists learn a lot by experimenting, or trying things out. Try things for yourself. A scientist takes nothing for granted. He may be sure an idea is true. Still, he always tests it, if he can, to make certain he is right.

If you have learned some of these things already, you will be ahead. Maybe you learned them in school or by reading.

COMPLETE THESE THREE REQUIREMENTS:

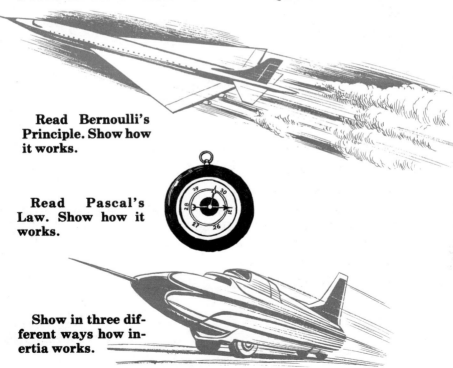

Read Bernoulli's Principle. Show how it works.

Read Pascal's Law. Show how it works.

Show in three different ways how inertia works.

- Show the effects of atmospheric pressure.

- Show the effects of air pressure.

- Show the effects of water and air pressure.

- Explain what causes fog. Show how this works.

- Explain how crystals are formed. Make some.

- Define balance. Show three different balancing tricks.

- Show in three different ways how your two eyes work together.

- Show what is meant by an optical illusion.

- Get a booklet on how to care for the eyes. Read it.

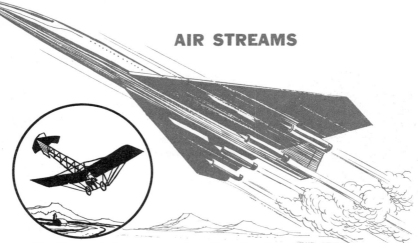

AIR STREAMS

In the 1700's a great family of scientists and mathematicians called Bernoulli lived in Switzerland. One of them, Daniel Bernoulli, discovered a fact that is known as Bernoulli's Principle.

He said something important about a stream of liquid or of a gas like air. The pressure is highest where the stream is slowest. In a water pipe, the water pressure is highest where the pipe is wide. Where the pipe is narrow, the pressure goes down.

Bernoulli's Principle explains how a plane can fly.

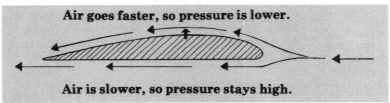

Air goes faster, so pressure is lower.

Air is slower, so pressure stays high.

The plane flies because the air travels longer *over* the wing. This causes lower pressure there. The air *under* the wing travels in a straight line, so its pressure stays high. The plane is lifted because of this difference in pressure.

Here are some ways for you to try out Bernoulli's Principle.

Lay a strip of newspaper about 6 by 22 inches over a bottle.
Blow under the bottle between the sheets of newspaper. The moving air stream makes low pressure between the paper sheets. The atmospheric pressure pushes them together.

Sit on the floor. Hold your mouth just above the edge of a table. Blow hard over a dime. Blow toward a point about 6 inches above the middle of a plate. The air stream will take the dime with it into the plate.

Hold a light bulb against your mouth. Hold a lighted match 1 or 2 inches beyond the bulb. Blow hard against the bulb, and the air stream will put out the match.

Put your mouth about 2 inches in front of three soup cans. Hold a lighted match about 2 inches beyond the cans. Blow hard against the cans and the match will go out.

Hold a lighted match in front of the middle of a funnel. Blow into the small end, and the flame will come toward you. Move the flame toward the top of the funnel. Watch the flame go away from you.

YOU CAN'T BLOW IT OFF

1. Push a pin through the middle of a 3-inch cardboard square.
2. Put the pin into the hole in a spool or Tinker Toy spool.
3. Put the spool to your mouth and blow steadily. The cardboard will stay on the spool. The harder you blow, the tighter it will hold.

The air stream makes a low-pressure area. It is between the cardboard and the bottom of the spool. The atmosphere pushes the cardboard against the spool.

Hold a lighted match behind a calling card and blow hard against the card. You will blow the flame toward you.

Fold each end of a piece of 4- by 8-inch writing paper 1 inch down. Set it on a table. Try to blow it over by blowing hard under it. You can't do it.

WEIGH AIR

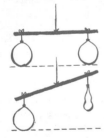

Make a simple scale with a stick and a loop of string. Blow up two balloons. Tie one with a bowknot. Slip the loops over the stick. Move the strings until they balance.

Let the air out of the tied balloon. The balloon with the air will settle down. The weight of its air pulled it down.

Drop a dime into a small funnel. Put your finger over the small end of the funnel. Blow down hard into the funnel on the side nearest you. The dime will pop out easily. Repeat with finger off the lower end of the funnel. Now, you can't lift it.

Blowing down increases the air pressure in the lower part of the funnel. The upward pressure raises the coin if you have plugged the bottom of the funnel.

COMPRESSED AIR

1. Make a ball of a 1-inch-square piece of newspaper.
2. Lay a pop bottle on its side on a table. Put the ball in the neck of the bottle.
3. Blow into the bottle. The ball will come out of the bottle.

The air you blow into the bottle increases the pressure. This drives the ball outward.

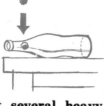

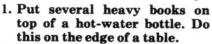

1. Put several heavy books on top of a hot-water bottle. Do this on the edge of a table.
2. Hold the opening of the bottle tightly against your mouth. Blow hard into the bottle. Your breath will lift the books.

1. Put a balloon into a glass. Have the bottom of the balloon touching the bottom of the glass.
2. Blow up the balloon. Hold it shut. You can lift the glass by the neck of the balloon.

The air pressure holds the balloon against the glass.

194

WATER PRESSURE and AIR PRESSURE

Because of science, men can work on the bottom of a river, lake, or sea. They use a diving bell. Air is fed into the bell through a hose. Air pressure keeps the water out. To show how this works:

1. Float a bottle cap in a bucket full of water.

2. Place a dry glass over the cap. Push the glass down halfway. The cap floats.

3. Push the diving bell (glass) to the bottom, the cap rests on the bottom.

4. Raise the glass carefully, the cap will float again.

To see how air pressure works against water pressure:

1. Slip a balloon onto a faucet. Fill it and support the weight.

2. Hold the neck tightly. Slip balloon off. Set it in the sink or a bucket of water. Let go of the neck. Air pressure pushing on the surface of the water forces the water out. It looks like a fountain.

195

PASCAL'S LAW

A French physicist named Blaise Pascal lived in the 1600's. He discovered a fact about liquids. If a liquid or a gas like air is in a closed container, pressure in every direction will be the same. When pressure is added to the top, pressure will increase allover the container.

To show Pascal's Law, try this experiment:

You will need a friend, a hot-water bottle, and a hose about 6 feet long. You will also need a funnel and a board 6 by 10 inches.

Hook up the funnel and the hose as shown. Put the board on top of the empty hot-water bottle. Hold the funnel about 5 feet above the floor. Pour water into it until the funnel is about half full. You may think that your friend's weight will keep the water from going into the bottle. It won't though. The water will go into the bottle. What's more, it will lift your friend.

Raise and lower the funnel several times. What happens?

This shows how a hydraulic press lifts your family's car in a service station. Then, of course, the mechanic can work on the underside of it.

Here are some more experiments showing how pressure works on a liquid.

1. Punch pinholes in the middle of a balloon.
2. Fill the balloon with water—all jets are the same length.

1. Punch five holes near the bottom of a tall juice can. Make them about one-half to three-quarters of an inch apart.
2. Fill the can with water. Notice that all the streams are the same length.

1. Punch three holes in a tall juice can. Put the first hole near the bottom. Make the others about 1 inch apart and a little to one side.
2. Fill the can with water. Notice the difference in the streams. The longest is at the bottom. The shortest is at the top.

This proves something about water pressure. At any point, it is in proportion to that point's depth below the water's surface.

1. Use a can with a lid that can be taken off. Punch a nail hole in the lid. Make another hole near the bottom of the can.
2. Fill the can with water. Put the lid on.
3. Turn the can over and water will run out of the hole in the lid.
4. Put your finger over the hole in the side and the water stops. Remove your finger and it starts.

Your finger stops the air coming in. There is then no pressure of the atmosphere above the water. The upward force of atmosphere on the water in the bottom hole keeps the water from running out.

BUOYANCY OF LIQUIDS

THE LAW OF ARCHIMEDES

Archimedes was a Greek philosopher and scientist. He lived almost 2,000 years ago. He found that anything solid that is put in a liquid is held up. It is held up by a force equal to the weight of the liquid that it displaces. If you drop something into water, the water level rises. The object seems to weigh less. It is being pushed up by a force equal to the weight of the water displaced.

Here are things you can do to test this law:

Put a fresh egg in a glass of water. The egg sinks to the bottom. The weight of water it displaces is less than its own weight.

Dissolve a heaping tablespoon of salt in a glass of fresh water. The egg now floats. It is at a depth where it displaces salt water weighing the same as the egg.

Pour out half of the salt water. Put the glass down. When the water that is left is still, set a spoon near the surface. Carefully pour freshwater into it until the glass is full once more. Take out the spoon and put the egg in the glass. It will float down halfway. There it displaces a combined fresh and salt water weight the same as its own.

1 Fill a quart-size soda bottle to the very top with water.
2 Put a medicine dropper in the bottle. Adjust water in dropper so it just barely floats.
3 Put in a cork. When you push down, the dropper will sink.

The dropper sinks because pressure on the cork squeezes the air in it. It takes in water. It sinks until the weight of the water it displaces is less than the dropper's own weight.

4 When you raise the cork, the dropper will rise.

Air in the dropper expands and drives out the water. The dropper rises until the weight of the water it displaces is less than its own weight.

1 Add 3 teaspoonfuls of vinegar to a glass of water.
2 Using a dry spoon, put a heaping teaspoonful of baking soda into another glass. Add the vinegar water.
3 The gas bubbles are carbon dioxide (CO_2). When fizzing stops, add a quarter of a teaspoon of tiny seeds or coffee grounds.
4 Each becomes a little diver. Watch them as they grab a pearl and rise with it to the top. They let it go there and dive down again.

THE REASON: Displacement again—or maybe they just like pearls!

RAISIN DIVERS

1. Cut a raisin into four pieces and drop them into a glass of soda. They will sink to the bottom.
2. Soon the raisin divers will rise to the surface. Then they will dive to the bottom. They will rise and dive time after time.
3. Take a good look at the raisins. Notice the gas bubbles attached to each.
4. Raisins and gas bubbles rise after their combined weight becomes less than the weight of the water they displace. When enough gas bubbles escape, the raisins sink to the bottom of the glass again.

Other divers can be made from very small bottles.

To make a diver out of a small bottle:

1. Put it open end down into a glass of water. Tilt it to get the air out. Do this until the top of the bottle is just under the surface of the water.
2. Cover the mouth of the bottle with your finger. Put it in a milk bottle full of water. Remove your finger underwater.
3. Put the palm of your hand over the mouth of the milk bottle. Push down. The bottle will dive.
4. Let up on your hand. The bottle will rise.

1. Put two glasses upside down in a pail of water. One glass should be full of water. The other should contain air. Be sure that each has its open end underwater.
2. Tip the glass with air under the glass with water. The air will run uphill into the glass of water.
3. Now pour it back into the first glass.

1. Cut both ends out of a food can. Cut a piece of cardboard slightly larger than the diameter of the can.
2. Hold the cardboard under the bottom of the can. Push cardboard and can just under the surface of the water.
3. Take away your hand. The cardboard will hold against the bottom of the can and keep the inside dry.
4. Carefully pour water into the can. The cardboard will hold until the water level is the same inside as outside.
5. Try this with another cardboard that has a hole in it. You'll have a small fountain, like a hole in the bottom of a boat.

FOG

1. Fill a bottle with hot water. Then pour out most of the water. Leave about 1 inch in the bottom.
2. Hold it to the light. Notice the streams of vapor rising from the bottle.
3. Put an ice cube in the bottle opening. Hold it toward the light. Notice the thin streams of vapor moving down into the bottle.

When cold air cools warm, moist air, the water molecules form small drops of water. Millions of these drops make a cloud or fog.

1. Put about 1 inch of cold water in a quart-sized bottle.
2. Cover the opening with your hand. Shake hard to soak the air in the bottle. Pour out the water. Hold the bottle firmly upside down.
3. Light a wooden match. Quickly blow it out. Put the smoking head into the opening of the bottle. The smoke will help the water vapor change into waterdrops.
4. Set the bottle in a good light. Place your mouth on the bottle opening. Press down and blow hard—you'll then see clear air in the bottle.
5. Raise your head. The fog forms again. Blowing helps to heat the air. This evaporates the fog you can see.

When you raise your head, the compressed air expands and cools. Cooling condenses water vapor into tiny waterdrops you can see. Thus the fog forms in the bottle again.

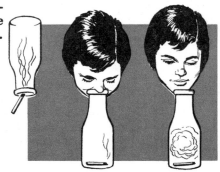

ATMOSPHERIC PRESSURE

The earth's atmosphere is many miles deep. At sea level, it is almost 15 pounds of pressure per square inch. This pressure is on everything.

Here are things you can do to test your own air or atmospheric pressure:

POP-IN

1. Cook an egg in boiling water for 10 minutes.
2. Put it in cold water. Take off the shell.
3. Fold a small piece of newspaper three times in the same direction.
4. Light it. Drop it into a bottle. Quickly put the egg in the top of the bottle.
5. The egg will bounce up and down. Then it will slip neatly into the bottle.

The burning paper expands the air, pushing most of it out. The air coming out makes the egg bounce. When the air that's left in the bottle cools, the inside pressure drops. The outside pressure pushes egg into the bottle.

POP-OUT
1. Wash out the burned paper.
2. Push the top of the bottle against your mouth. Bend your head back and blow hard into the bottle.
3. Remove your mouth and the egg will pop out.

Air blown into the bottle goes around the egg. It increases the air pressure in the bottle. This pushes the egg out.

1. Pour the water from a half-filled bottle into a pan. Set a 2-inch-high candle in the pan and light it.
2. Hold the empty bottle over the candle until the bubbling stops. Have the top a little below the water.
3. Lower the bottle. The candle and water will rise up in the bottle.

The candle flame expands the air, pushing part of it out. The air pressure in the bottle is cut down. The atmospheric pressure on the water pushes it up into the bottle. The flame goes out when it burns up all of the oxygen in the bottle.

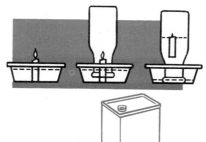

Pour a glass of water into an empty screw-top (gallon) can. Put the open can on a stove. Leave the top off. Boil the water. Let it steam for a minute or more.

Use a hot pad. Take the can off the stove. Screw on the cap. Turn the can over and place, top down, into a pail of water. The can will be crushed.

The steam drives nearly all of the air out. The water cools the steam, leaving the can almost empty. The atmospheric pressure crushes the can.

1. Fill a large round balloon with water and tie it. Place in an empty bucket.
2. Light a folded piece of paper. Drop it into a bottle. Quickly press the top of the bottle against the balloon.

The atmospheric pressure pushes the balloon up into the bottle.

Light a folded piece of paper. Drop into a bottle. Tip the bottle on its side. Push your hand against the top of the bottle. You will feel it drawn into the bottle.

Suck air out of a bottle. Stop the bottle with your tongue. You will find that the bottle will hang on your tongue.

1. Make a cork boat as shown. Float it.
2. Put a glass over it. Slowly turn the glass bottom up.
3. Raise the glass, but keep the top underwater.

INERTIA

Inertia is another way of saying "Do not disturb." A thing at rest wants to remain at rest. A thing in motion wants to remain in motion in the same straight line. Try these experiments:

1. Set a coin on a card on the top of a bottle. Snap the edge of the card. It will fly out and the coin will drop in the bottle.

2. Make a stack of nickels. Snap a penny along the table at the bottom coin. The bottom nickel will fly out; the others remain in a stack.

3. Set a glass of water on the end of a long strip of paper. Pull the paper slowly. The glass moves with it. Give the paper a sudden jerk. The glass stands still.

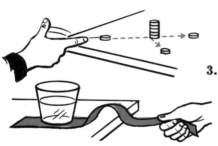

4. Spin a fresh egg on its side. It will stop soon. Spin a hard-boiled egg. It will spin for a much longer time. When you spin a fresh egg, you spin the outside. The white and yolk inside are loose. They want to remain at rest. When you spin the hard-boiled egg, you spin the whole thing. The insides are solid.

Swing a pail of water back and forth at arm's length. After a few times, swing it over your head in a full circle.

TELL WHAT HAPPENS. DO YOU KNOW WHY?

206

CRYSTALS

Heat water until it is slightly more than lukewarm. Stir alum into it until no more dissolves. Set aside to cool. When crystals have formed, pick out largest ones. Add to solution as much more alum as is represented by the crystals you removed. Heat gently until all is dissolved. Cool. Pour cooled solution into narrow glass. Tie thread to largest crystal you picked. Hang this in solution. Place in quiet spot. Let crystal grow for 3 days. Try it with epsom salt, sugar, and table salt: both iodized and plain.

BALANCE

The whole body moves to balance itself when we move. Here are some things that show what happens when you can't balance.

1. Stand with your heels and shoulders against the wall. Drop a cloth about a foot in front of you. Try to pick it up without moving your feet or bending your knees.

   The faster you try to bend, the harder you will fall.

2. Place a chair against the wall. Bend over it with your head touching the wall. Move your feet back. Your legs, from ankles to hips, should slant toward the wall. Lift the chair. Try to stand straight without moving your feet.

3. Stand with one shoulder, arm, leg, and foot close against a wall. Try to bring the outside foot up to touch the one next to the wall. You will fall. Lack of balance is the cause.

The center of gravity of any body is the center of its weight.

Make a figure out of two corks. Put in a piece of coat-hanger wire bent as shown. Slide spool on the lower end of the wire. Bend up to hold it. Place on the edge of a table. He will bow and balance on one leg or two.

Cut a bird out of a 6- by 3-inch piece of light cardboard. Glue or tape a penny at the front end of each wing. The middle of each penny should be just in front of the bird's beak. Set the beak on the end of your finger. Or put it on the corner of a table or a book. It won't fall.

OPTICAL ILLUSIONS

Your eyes are truly wonderful instruments. They send your brain pictures of all that you see. Care for them. Protect them. They get tired when you sit too close to TV and watch it too long. Reading in a poor light is harmful. So is staring at the sun.

We haven't enough pages in this book to tell all about eyes. All we want is to start you thinking about them. If you are interested, you can find out more about them on your own.

Some people say seeing is believing. Can this be? Sometimes our eyes make us see holes in our hands or see double. They can make shapes change. We see things not there. We don't judge sizes right.

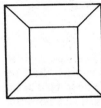

◀ Draw a ½-inch square inside a 1-inch square. Connect the corners. The inside square seems to move closer, then farther away.

Draw a box as shown. ▶ Look at it steadily. Sometimes you seem to be looking at the top of the box. Sometimes it seems to be the bottom.

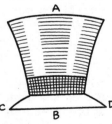

◀ Is the high silk hat longer from A to B than from C to D? Measure it.

Try putting a dime on top of this box so the coin won't touch the edges. Try it! ▶

Which of the two designs at right is longer? Better get out your ruler. ▶

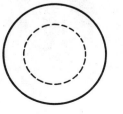

◀ Which of the dotted circles is larger?

Roll a sheet of paper into a tube. Hold the edge of your hand against it. Then look through the tube with one eye. Look at your hand with the other eye. There seems to be a hole in your hand.

When your eyes see something, they work together. They turn to bring the two pictures to the same parts of the retinas. Nerves carry the pictures on your retinas to your brain. Your brain makes one picture out of the two.

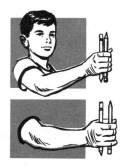

SEEING DOUBLE

Hold two pencils, as shown, at arm's length. Look past the pencils at the far corner of the room. You will see two sets of pencils. Do this again with the pencils held about 1 inch apart. You will see four pencils.

Place the tips of two fingers together about 6 inches from your eyes. Look past them at the far corner of the room and you will see a small sausage. Pull the fingers apart slowly. The sausage will seem to hang in the air.

Stand in a corner of the room with your back to the light. Look in a mirror. Notice the size of the opening in the pupil of each eye.

They will be large. Face a light. Look in the mirror again. They will be small.

Look at something far away. Cup your hands into tubes. Look through them as you would through field glasses. You see more clearly because your pupils get bigger. They receive more light from the objects when they are protected from other light.

SCIENTIST
SCOREBOARD

Requirements

Approved
by

SHOWMAN

Does your pack need some entertainment? You will be a handy boy to have around if you have your Showman badge. This tells others that you know a lot about puppets, music, or plays.

What's more, it's lots of fun to earn if you enjoy any of these things.

Don't let the requirements scare you. You CAN write a play for puppets or for real actors. It probably won't be ready for Broadway. But, those who see it will love it. And so will you!

The Showman activity badge will teach you to speak well. You will learn a lot about the theater and music. But mostly it's just for fun.

Ready now? On with the show!

To earn the Showman badge, do four tests for any one of the following: Puppetry, Music, or Drama.

PUPPETRY

COMPLETE FOUR OF THE FOLLOWING:

- Write a puppet play about one of your Webelos den activities.

- Make a set of fist puppets or marionettes for the play you have written.

- Build a simple stage for fist puppets, shadow puppets, or marionettes.

- Alone or with the help of others, put on a show for your den or pack.

- Make a bib puppet and put on a one-man show with it.

- Make a set of paper bag puppets for a barbershop quartet. With the help of three others harmonize.

- There are fist, shadow, finger, and bib puppets. There are paper bag puppets, stick puppets, and marionettes. Show their differences using ones you have made.

FIST PUPPET

PAPER BAG PUPPET

FINGER PUPPET

STICK PUPPET

MARIONETTE

BIB PUPPET

SHADOW PUPPET

213

THE PLAY

Writing a puppet play about one of your Webelos den activities is really quite simple. All you have to do is write down the answers to a few questions.

1. Where were you going?
- To the old battlefield.

2. What were you going to do?

- Study the old battlefield and figure out why they fought the way they did.

3. Who was to do what?

- Bill and Jim were to bring the lunch. Joe was to carry the flag. Woody was to bring the lemonade. Don the map-making stuff. Alec the tent.

4. What happened?

- Jim got his head stuck in the cannon.

5. How did you handle this hard problem?

- Bill suggested we light the fuse and fire the cannon.

- Woody wanted to build a fire under the cannon and melt the fathead out.

- We pulled and tugged. We tied a rope around his waist and lifted. We wiggled him from side to side.

- Alec shook some pepper down the barrel and Jim sneezed his way out.
6. Then what did you do?
- We made Jim our prisoner. We tied him to a tree for safekeeping.
- We pitched our headquarters tent.
- We spread out the map and followed the two armies' progress on it. Then we located the battle lines in the park.
- We figured the war could have been 2 years shorter. But the other side would have won.

STAGE

One of the most practical stages for hand puppets is the simple six-panel screen shown. It folds into an easily carried bundle about 2½ by 3 feet in size.

The sections on each side are 2½ feet wide. A stage opening 16 inches high by 2 feet wide is big enough.

The booth in the drawing can be made of 1- by 2-inch white pine. It hinges in the middle of the front section. The top half folds forward face to face. When it is set up, pin hinges hold the side sections in position.

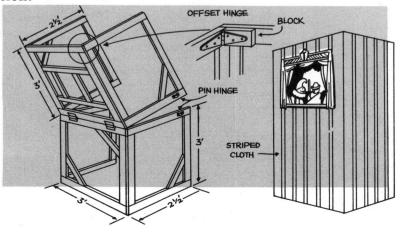

MUSIC

COMPLETE ANY FOUR OF THE FOLLOWING:

- Play four tunes on any band or orchestra instrument. Read these from music.

- Sing two songs alone or with a group.

- Make a collection of three or more records. Tell what you like about each one.

- Tell what folk music is. Hum, sing, or play a folk tune on a musical instrument.

- Name three American composers. Name the most famous work of each.

- Draw a staff. Draw on it a clef, sharp, flat, natural, note, and rest. Tell what each is used for.

- Show by beating or playing the difference between 2/4, 3/4, and 4/4 time.

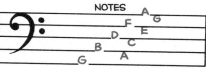

SHARP   FLAT   NATURAL   NOTES

TREBLE CLEF

BASS CLEF

NOTES

THREE AMERICAN COMPOSERS

Stephen Foster (1826-1864)

Writer of sad, sentimental, and humorous songs.

His songs:

- "Jeanie With the Light Brown Hair"
- "Old Folks at Home"
- "My Old Kentucky Home"
- "Oh! Susanna"
- "Beautiful Dreamer"

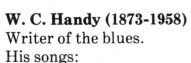

Victor Herbert (1859-1924)

Composer for operettas.

His best operettas:

- "Naughty Marietta"
- "The Red Mill"
- "The Viceroy"
- "The Fortune Teller"

W. C. Handy (1873-1958)

Writer of the blues.

His songs:

- "Memphis Blues"
- "Beale Street Blues"
- "St. Louis Blues"

THREE MORE AMERICAN COMPOSERS

George Gershwin (1898-1937)
Writer of popular songs, folk opera, and jazz compositions.
His works:
    "Porgy and Bess,"
      a folk opera
    "Rhapsody in Blue"
    "Concerto in F"
Songs:
    "Swanee"
    "Do It Again"

Aaron Copland (born 1900)
Writer of symphonies, concertos, and ballets.
His works:
    "Symphony for Organ and
      Orchestra"
    "Appalachian Spring"
    "Billy the Kid"
    "El Salon Mexico"

**Leonard Bernstein
(born 1918)**
Composer for musical stage, symphonies.
His works:
    "West Side Story"
    "Wonderful Town"
    "Fancy Free"
    "Jeremiah"
    "Mass"

FOLK MUSIC

Folk music used to mean songs and tunes going back deep in a country's past. They told of the joys and sorrows of the people living then. They were funny too. Many American folk songs began in the countries from which our settlers first came.

Folk music is becoming more popular all the time. Songs have been composed in the folk music manner. These are accepted now as folk tunes.

If you don't know any folk music, you have fun ahead of you. See if you can get a folk song book from your library. Learn a few.

MUSIC SYMBOLS

The sixth and seventh projects ask for music training. Perhaps you are lucky enough to be studying music with a teacher. If so, probably you can do them. If not, find out about them. The things mentioned in these projects are easy for those who can read music. Learn what they mean. Ask your music teacher in school for help.

DRAMA

COMPLETE ANY FOUR
OF THE FOLLOWING:

- Give a monologue on a patriotic, humorous, or holiday subject.
- Attend a play. Describe the story. Tell what you liked about it.
- Read a play. Make a model stage setting for one of the acts.
- Write, put on, and take part in a one-act play.
- Make a list of stage directions. Tell what they mean.
- Describe a theater-in-the-round. What are its good and bad points?
- Tell the difference between an opera and a light opera. Tell how a musical and a dramatic play are different.
- Read a story about Shakespeare. Draw a picture of his theater.

PLAYS TO READ

Do you want to write a play for either puppets or actors? You may find it helpful to read a few plays. You'll enjoy reading them, even if you don't write one.

Get one or two books from your library. Notice that the person who writes plays is not just a storyteller. When you read a story, your imagination fills in the details. That isn't true with plays. The list of characters, their dress, and the setting must be described carefully beforehand. This is so that actors can bring the play to life.

The lines that the actors speak are usually printed in regular type. The directions for their actions are set off differently. They are usually in italics. Maybe your pack library has a copy of *Skits and Puppets.* It has many funny skits to read or put on.

MONOLOGUE

A single actor recites or acts out a monologue. It can be a poem, a story, or an essay. It may be on a serious subject, such as patriotism. It may just be a funny story.

You can make a monologue out of almost any poem or story. Sometimes monologues have more than one character. Then you must play all parts.

Here's an example of a funny monologue to be acted out by just one boy.

THE STORY

Ladies and gentlemen, three of us were going to put on a play tonight. The other two boys haven't come yet. I'll have to take all of the parts myself. The name of the play is "Cub Scout Inspection." The cast of characters is the den mother, the den chief, and Johnny. Johnny's a Cub Scout wearing one red and one blue sock. The scene is a Cub Scout den meeting. The den mother is speaking.

Den Mother: Cubs, line up for inspection.
Den Chief: They all look fine except Johnny.
Johnny: Me?
Den Mother: Johnny?
Den Chief: Yes, Johnny.
Johnny: What's wrong with me?
Den Mother: What's wrong with him?
Den Chief: Look at his socks.
Johnny: My socks?
Den Mother: His socks?
Den Chief: Your socks.
Den Mother: Why Johnny, you have on one red sock . . .
Den Chief: . . . and one blue sock.
Johnny: One red sock?
Den Chief: Yes, and one blue sock.
Johnny: That's funny.
Den Chief: What's funny?
Den Mother: What's funny?
Johnny: I have another pair at home just like them.

STAGE SETTING

The third project asks you to read a play. Then you are to make a model stage setting for one of the acts. This means making a small model—perhaps 2 feet wide and 1 foot high. It should show how the stage should look for that act.

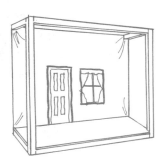

Keep it simple. Remember, the audience comes to the theater ready to use imagination. Therefore, you don't need to fill in every detail. It doesn't have to be true to life, either.

First, make a simple frame. Hang a piece of cloth—not brightly colored—from the rear for a backdrop. On it you can paint or pin some simple scenery. If it's an outdoor scene, just make a couple of paper trees and color them. Pin them on the backdrop. You can do the same thing for windows and doors for an indoor scene.

For furniture, borrow stuff from your sister's dollhouse. Read the play carefully before deciding where to put your props. Don't clutter the scene with things that won't be used. If there are three actors in the act, you don't need six chairs. The action will tell you what to do.

WRITING A PLAY

Probably you have helped out or taken part in play-acting before. Perhaps it was in school or in your den.

Just helping out isn't enough to earn the Showman badge in drama. You must do any four of the eight things listed. Why not write, put on, and take part in a one-act play? You can tell how you feel about places and people this way. You can do it in a serious or funny way.

When you have written your play, read it over two or three times. Do the characters talk too much or too little? Is the conversation one-sided? Or do the characters talk to one another naturally as you do with your friends?

To move the plot along, all the talk must be related directly to the story.

Drop every speech or remark that doesn't help the play. Try to keep it moving by tying the scenes together. Too many changes can bore an audience.

Keep your characters simple. Make them act the same way all the time. A character should be either good or bad, kind or evil, all the way through the play.

Don't use long speeches. Make the talk natural. Use exaggerated gestures and pantomime freely.

Finally, save something for the end. It could be something funny to send your audience away laughing. Or it could be serious to send them home thinking.

STAGE DIRECTIONS

As a producer and director, you will have to give stage directions. When you reread your play, think about what each character does. Note where each stands or sits, and where he moves in your script.

Here is an easy way to learn stage directions. Make a floor plan of the scene, like the one in the drawing.

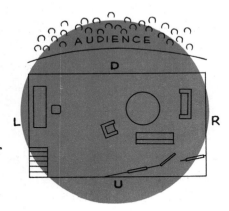

URC. Up right center
UC. Up center
ULC. Up left center
RC. Right center
C. Center
LC. Left center
DRC. Down right center
DC. Down center
DLC. Down left center

Keep the scene balanced at all times. For example, perhaps you will move one actor to the right or to the left. Then, move another to balance the scene.

THEATER-IN-THE-ROUND

Two main kinds of stages are used today. One is the proscenium stage. It is the kind you usually think of when you hear the word "stage." It's just a platform, usually raised, at one end of the room. There is a curtain which can be opened or closed. Probably, this is what you have in your school.

The other kind of stage is called theater-in-the-round. It's also known as arena theater or central staging.

In a theater-in-the-round, the stage is in the center of the room. The audience sits around all sides of it. There is no curtain.

It is very good for plays with small casts and close-up action. The audience feels very close to the players. The actors go on and leave the stage along aisles through the audience. Instead of a curtain, the theater is darkened between scenes or acts. Then the scenery is moved.

For plays with a large cast or bold action, theater-in-the-round is not good. The audience is too close to the stage. Many actors moving about or a great deal of fast action can be confusing.

OPERA AND MUSICALS

Opera and musicals are a lot alike. But there are some differences.

Both are plays with music. Usually, the opera will have a serious plot, and the musical will be cheerful. The opera's music will be "classical" and the musical's music will be "popular." But there are different kinds of operas, some quite a bit like musicals. Here are the types of operas:

- Grand Opera: The plot is serious, and all the story is sung by the actor-singers.
- Light Opera: The plot will not be serious—in fact, it can be very funny. Some of the story may be spoken rather than sung.
- Operetta: There really isn't much of a plot at all. The music is cheerful. Some of the story is spoken.

A musical can be very much like an operetta. A great deal of the plot unfolds in dialogue. It usually is bright and cheerful. Generally, the orchestra for a musical can be much smaller than that for an opera. The reason is that the music is not as hard for either the singers or musicians.

SHOWMAN SCOREBOARD

Do four tests for any one of the following: Puppetry, Music, or Drama

PUPPETRY **DO FOUR:**

- Write a puppet play about one of your Webelos den activities.   214

———————

- Make a set of fist puppets or marionettes for the play you have written.   213

———————

- Build a simple stage for fist puppets, shadow puppets, or marion ettes.   215

———————

- Alone or with the help of others, put on a show for your den or pack.

———————

- Make a bib puppet and put on a one-man show with it.   213

———————

- Make a set of paper bag puppets for a barbershop quartet. With the help of three others harmonize.   213

- There are fist, shadow, finger, and bib puppets. There are paper bag puppets, stick puppets, and marionettes. Show their differences using ones you mave made.   213

———————

MUSIC **DO FOUR:**

- Play four tunes on any band or orchestra instrument. Read these from music.

- Sing two songs alone or with a group.

- Make a collection of three or more

records. Tell what you like about
each one.

- Tell what folk music is. Hum, sing,
or play a folk tune on a musical instrument.   219
- Name three American composers.
Name the most famous work of
each.   217
- Draw a staff. Draw on it a clef,
sharp, flat, natural, note, and rest.
Tell what each is used for.   216
- Show by beating or playing the
difference between 2/4, 3/4, and
4/4 time.   219

DRAMA   **DO FOUR:**

- Give a monologue on a patriotic,
humorous, or holiday subject.   221
- Attend a play. Describe the story.
Tell what you liked about it.
- Read a play. Make a model stage
setting for one of the acts.   223
- Write, put on, and take part in a
one-act play.   224
- Make a list of stage directions.
Tell what they mean.   225
- Describe a theater-in-the-round.
What are its good points and bad
points?   226
- Tell the difference between an
opera and a light opera. Tell how
a musical and a dramatic play are
different.   227
- Read a story about Shakespeare.
Draw a picture of his theater.

SPORTSMAN

America is a sports-loving country. Large crowds come out to see high school and college teams play football and basketball. Big league baseball and professional football draw many people.

These games are great fun to watch. But too many Americans are watchers rather than players. Be a player. You will find that playing a game is more fun than just watching it.

Try many sports. Not everyone can be a great baseball or football player. But if you are willing to practice, you can become very good in other sports. Take your choice—swimming, boating, badminton, horseshoes, canoeing—try one or more.

This book will tell you something about some of these sports and others. There is not enough room to explain all about them. Talk with players in the sports you want to try. Watch them play. Above all, play yourself.

TO QUALIFY FOR THIS BADGE:

- Show the signals used by referees in football, basketball, or baseball.
- Pick and do the requirements for TWO INDIVIDUAL and TWO TEAM sports.

YOU MUST
- Be familiar with the skills or techniques.
- Know the rules, the courtesies, and how to score.
- Know the equipment used and how to care for it.
- Know the safety rules.
- Demonstrate or take part to a reasonable degree.

You may use any recognized individual or team sports to earn this badge. Listed below are a few examples:

TEAM SPORTS	INDIVIDUAL SPORTS	
Baseball	Skiing	Bowling
Softball	Swimming	Tennis
Basketball	Ice-skating	Golf
Volleyball	Boating	Badminton
Soccer	Roller-skating	Table tennis
	Fishing	Horseshoes
	Archery	Shuffleboard

BASEBALL

The Positions

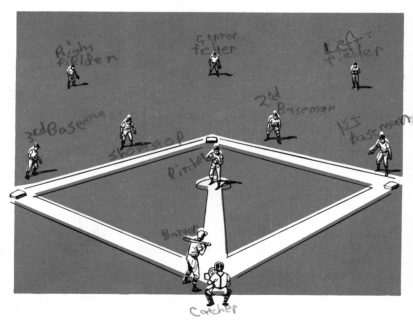

BATS

- Keep your bat dry. Water-soaked bats lose their spring.
- Don't hit rocks with a bat.
- Use one that feels good when you swing. If you are swinging late, try a lighter bat.

GLOVES

- If your glove gets wet during a game, dry it off completely afterward.
- Once or twice a season, rub it with neat's-foot oil. That keeps the leather from cracking.

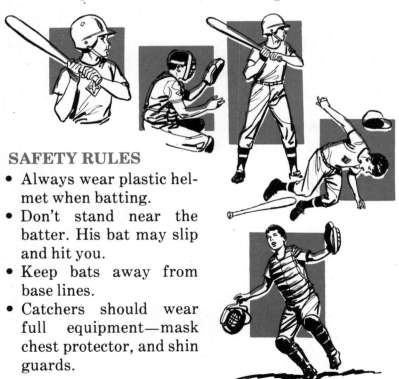

SAFETY RULES

- Always wear plastic helmet when batting.
- Don't stand near the batter. His bat may slip and hit you.
- Keep bats away from base lines.
- Catchers should wear full equipment—mask chest protector, and shin guards.

THE GAME

Probably you have played enough baseball at school or a playground to know the rules. It is a game of three skills—running, throwing, and batting. Practice all three. Try to play all of the positions to see which one suits you best.

This chart may help you decide which position is best for you to play:

IF YOU ARE A:		
Fast runner	**Good thrower**	**Good batter**
YOUR BEST POSITION MAY BE:		
Outfielder Shortstop 2d baseman	Outfielder Pitcher Catcher Shortstop 3d baseman	*Any position but especially* Outfielder 1st baseman 3d baseman

SOFTBALL

Probably, you have played this game too. It is almost the same as a baseball game on a smaller field.

Here are other differences:

• The ball is larger than a baseball.

• The barrel of the bat is thinner.

• The pitcher must throw the ball underhand.

PITCHING IN SOFTBALL

BASKETBALL

This is your game if you enjoy trying to outsmart another player. It is a team game, of course. But also, each player tries to "shake loose" from the one guarding him. He wants to take a shot.

SHOOTING

Practice shooting baskets from everywhere on the floor. Try all kinds of shots. You may be good at one kind, but practice them all. Then you will have a chance to score anywhere near the basket.

PASSING

This is the key to winning basketball. Always look for a player on your team near the basket. Try to get the ball to him so that he can shoot a basket.

Here are the three basic passes:

Two-handed   **Baseball throw**   **Bounce pass**

DRIBBLING

Learn to control the ball with your fingertips. Don't slap at it. Practice changing directions quickly. Learn to dribble without watching the ball.

TIPS FOR DEFENSE

- Stay between your man and the basket.
- Keep your eye on both the ball and the man you are guarding.
- On rebounds, try to block out players on the other team — without pushing them. Pushing is a foul.

EQUIPMENT AND SAFETY RULES

- Wear clean socks and well-fitting sneakers.
- The court should be clean and dry to keep players from slipping.
- Indoors, if walls are near end lines, they should be padded with gym mats.

VOLLEYBALL

This is a fine team game to learn. It is fun, and you will be able to play it all your life.

You may never have played volleyball before, so we will explain the game.

Each team has six players. (But it can be played for fun with a few more or less.) The teams hit the ball back and forth across the net. They use both fists and open hands. They try to keep the ball from touching the floor on their side and to return it back over the net.

Each team may hit it one, two, or three times on their side. No player may hit it twice in a row. Only the serving team scores points. When they don't score, the other team gets the serve.

Points are scored, or the serve changes hands,
WHEN:
- The ball hits the court.
- One team hits it more than three times before it goes over the net.
- The ball goes out of bounds. (It is a penalty for the team that touched it last. If on the serving team, it loses the serve. If on the other team, it scores a point.)
- A player catches instead of hits the ball.

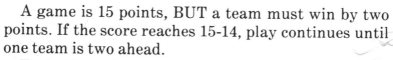

A game is 15 points, BUT a team must win by two points. If the score reaches 15-14, play continues until one team is two ahead.

Each time the serve changes hands, the players move one position clockwise. The server is the player in the right back position. There is a new server each time the serve changes hands.

Good players learn to "set it up" and to "spike it." One forward taps the ball high right in front of the net. Another forward jumps as high as he can. He hits the ball hard down over the net into the other team's court. The "spike" is hard to return.

INDIVIDUAL SPORTS

There are many sports that you can enjoy alone or against only one other player. We call them individual sports.

You may have tried some of these sports as a Wolf or Bear Cub Scout. They were in the electives for those ranks. They were skiing, swimming, ice-skating, boating, roller-skating, archery, tennis, and fishing.

If you want to do the Webelos requirements for one of those sports, you can. But you should be better than before. You should know a lot more now.

There are other fine sports you might try. Here are a few of them.

BOWLING

The idea is to roll a ball down the alley and knock over 10 pins. They are set up in a triangle. They are wooden and 15 inches high. The balls weigh from 10 to 16 pounds. They have two or three finger holes.

A bowler knocking down all the pins on his first try has a "strike." If the pins don't all go down, he rolls another ball. If this one knocks over the rest, it's a "spare." If they do not all fall this time, it's a "miss."

A game is 10 "frames" for each player. On the 10th frame, if he gets a strike, he rolls two more balls. If he gets a spare, he rolls one more.

SCORING

A strike is an extra count of 10. Add it to the pins knocked down with the next two balls. A spare also counts 10. Add it to the pins knocked over by the next ball. For a miss, just score the pins that fell. Ask someone at the bowling alley to help you.

When a bowler makes a strike the scorer uses this mark in the little box: ⊠

For a spare, he makes ⊡ . For a miss ⊟ . For a split, or very hard shot when the pins left standing are far apart ⊙ . If the bowler makes this hard shot, he writes: ⊘ .

GOLF

Golf is a popular game among adults. Not many boys your age play it. Clubs are costly. They need to fit your size. As you grow, you'll need new ones. Maybe your mother has clubs that she will share with you. Your father's clubs will be too big for you. At the start you could get by with about five clubs. Later you'll want more.

The idea is to hit the ball into the hole with the fewest shots.

The "woods" are for long shots and the "irons" are for shorter ones. Most golf courses have either 9 or 18 holes. A "round" might be either number.

Each shot in golf is played a little differently. Here are some general rules:

- Keep your head down and your eyes on the ball till your club hits it.
- On your backswing, keep your left arm straight on all shots. (Right arm if you're left-handed.)
- For long shots, have your feet spread comfortably. On short shots, put them closer together.

THE PROPER GRIP

DRIVING

ADDRESSING
THE BALL

BACKSWING...

**IRON
SHOTS**

CLUB MEETS
BALL...

PUTTING

FOLLOW
THROUGH...

RULES AND COURTESIES

- Play the ball where it lands. If it goes into a brook or gets lost in the woods, drop another ball. Then add one stroke to your score.
- Don't talk when another player is shooting.
- If golfers behind you are going faster than you are, let them "play through." That means go ahead.
- The golfer whose ball is farthest away from the hole shoots for the hole first.

BADMINTON

Badminton is a game you can play in your backyard. All you need is a net, two rackets, and a "bird."

The bird is hit in the air back and forth across the net. A point is scored when the bird touches the ground or goes out of bounds. A point is also scored if the bird is hit twice on the same side of the net.

THE COURT

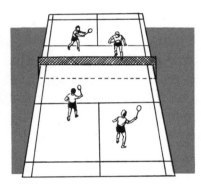

THE RULES

You will find a complete set of rules with your set. If you don't, ask the store where you bought it for the rules. Your dad or mother may have to help you read them. Play a game with them. With a little practice, you may be able to beat them.

TABLE TENNIS

You can have a lot of fun playing table tennis with your family or friends. The equipment doesn't cost much except for the table. Maybe you and your dad can make one.

The drawing shows the size of a table.

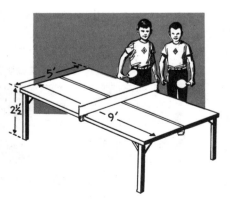

There should be room at both ends and the sides of the table. That way, players can move around easily. The net is 6 feet long. It sticks out 6 inches over each side of the table. Its top is 6 inches above the table.

You need two paddles (four for doubles) and a ball. (Better have more than one because they crunch when they are stepped on.) You can buy paddles, a net, and balls at any toy or sporting goods store.

The game begins with the server hitting the ball. It must bounce on his side of the net first. His opponent returns it back over the net so that it bounces there. It may bounce only once on each side. Play continues until one player hits the ball off the table or doesn't return it.

The first server keeps serving until five points have been scored. The other player then serves for five more points. The serve returns to the first player for five more. The one who reaches 21 first wins. BUT he must be two points ahead at the time. He must win by two.

With the score 20-20, it is called deuce. The game continues until one player is ahead by two. The serve changes hands after each point in a deuce game.

HOW TO GRIP THE PADDLE

THE SHAKEHANDS GRIP   THE PENHOLD GRIP

SHUFFLEBOARD

Here's a game that you may be able to play at home. Your family can have fun with it too. All that you need is a level concrete or blacktop driveway.

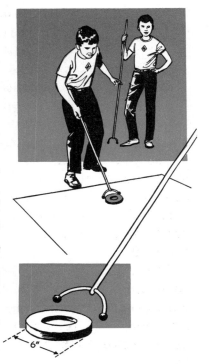

You can buy the equipment, or perhaps you and your dad can make it. If you are making it, cut out eight disks from wood, like this:
Paint four disks red and four of them black.
Make four pushing sticks, called cues, like this:

The size of the court is shown below. If you don't have enough room, don't let that stop you. Make the court to fit your space.

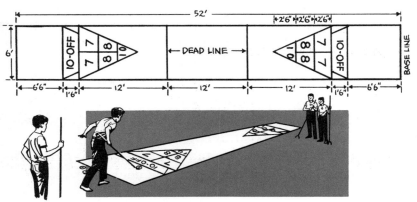

Now you're ready to play. The idea is to slide the disks from behind one base line toward the other triangle. They must land in one of the numbered spaces to score. Disks stopping on a line don't count. Disks which stop in the place marked "10 off" lose 10 points.

Either two or four persons can play. If two are playing, they start at the same end. One has the red disks, the other the black. They take turns pushing their disks.

You try to make your disks stop in the spaces marked 7, 8, or 10. You don't want them to go into the spaces marked "10 off." You also try to knock your opponent's disks out of the scoring spaces.

Disks are left on the court until all eight have been pushed. Those that don't reach the far Dead Line are taken off before the next shot. The players move to the other end. Then they shoot from there.

The game can be 50, 75, or 100.

The player scoring the highest on the last series of shots goes first next time.

When four people are playing, they play partners. One member of each team stays at each end.

OFFICIALS' SIGNALS

FOOTBALL

OFFSIDE

ILLEGAL PROCEDURE

ILLEGAL MOTION

ILLEGAL SHIFT

ILLEGAL RETURN

DELAY OF GAME

CLIPPING

ILLEGAL USE OF HANDS (HOLDING)

ILLEGALLY PASSING OR HANDLING BALL FORWARD

PASS INTERFERENCE

ROUGHING THE KICKER

INELIGIBLE RECEIVER DOWNFIELD

INCOMPLETE PASS— PENALTY DECLINED— NO PLAY— NO SCORE

TOUCHDOWN OR FIELD GOAL

TIME OUT

FIRST DOWN

START THE CLOCK

BASKETBALL

TIME OUT—FOUL

TECHNICAL FOUL

ILLEGAL USE OF HANDS

TRAVELING

HOLDING

PUSHING— CHARGING

ILLEGAL DRIBBLE

CANCEL SCORE

BASEBALL

STRIKE

BALL

OUT

SAFE

FAIR BALL
POINTS TOWARD OUTFIELD

FOUL BALL— POINTS AWAY FROM OUTFIELD

TIME OUT

TIME IN

SPORTSMAN SCOREBOARD

Requirements

**Approved
by**

RDL.
6.7 2/17/82

DO THESE:

- Show the signals used by referees in football, basketball, or baseball.   247
- Pick and do the requirements for TWO INDIVIDUAL and TWO TEAM sports.

YOU MUST:

- Be familiar with the skills or techniques.
- Know the rules, the courtesies, and how to score.
- Know the equipment used and how to care for it.
- Know the safety rules.
- Demonstrate or take part to a reasonable degree.   232

RDL.
6.7 7/17/82

You may use any recognized individual or team sports to earn this badge. Listed below are a few examples:

TEAM SPORTS	INDIVIDUAL SPORTS	
Baseball	✓Skiing	Bowling
Softball	Swimming	Tennis
Basketball	Ice-skating	Golf
✓Volleyball	Boating	Badminton
✓Soccer	✓Roller-skating	Table tennis
	Fishing	✓Horseshoes
	✓Archery	Shuffleboard

8/21/81 6.7

TRAVELER

Traveling is one of man's greatest adventures. Since time began, he has wanted to see new places. He HAD to know what was on the other side of the mountains. He floated down mighty rivers to see what he could find. He sailed across endless oceans in tiny ships. All of this in spite of terrible fears of the unknown. We still are traveling to unexplored areas. Now they are in our oceans' deeps and on the moon's surface and beyond.

Most of us would like to travel as the pioneers did through the wilds of America. Now you don't have the same kind of land to find and tame. Still, you do have a greater chance to travel than boys of the past did. You can see more, do more, and learn more. Why? Mostly because you can travel faster than ever before. Modern highways, railroads, and airways make this possible.

Why should you travel? Why not just stay where you were born and are growing up? Because you can discover new things, learn about new places, understand how our country grew. You can find out some things right on the spot about some of our country's history.

The important thing is to be interested. Some people really don't see or learn much at any time during their trip.

As you travel, ask questions. Find out about places along the way. Read signs about points of interest. Often you may learn of side trips. They may be worth leaving the main highways. When planning your trip, you might talk mom and dad into making some side trips. If not planned for, these sights will be missed.

Allow enough time to see, to explore, and to do things. All too often, vacation trips become rush trips. They are tiring instead of fun. One way to measure a good vacation is by how much is learned. The number of miles traveled isn't important.

251

More people are traveling today. Most families take a trip at least once a year. More of them than ever are tent and trailer camping. Often in the summer, state and national parks are filled up. Keep this in mind if you are planning to camp.

Read what you must do for the Traveler badge. As you complete these tests, you can learn a lot. You can find out about three kinds of transportation. They are bus, train, and plane. To qualify for this badge—

COMPLETE FIVE OF THE FOLLOWING:

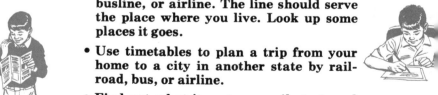

- **Get a map or timetable from a railroad, busline, or airline. The line should serve the place where you live. Look up some places it goes.**

- **Use timetables to plan a trip from your home to a city in another state by railroad, bus, or airline.**

- **Find out what it costs per mile to travel by bus, railroad, or plane.**

- **With your parents or guardian, take a trip to some place that interests you. Go by bus, boat, train, or plane.**

- **List four nearby trips you would like to take with your parents. Lay out the trips on a highway map of your state. Using that map, act as navigator on one of these trips. It should be at least 25 miles long and have six or more turns.**

- **Pack a suitcase for a trip.**

- **Check the first aid kit in the family car.**

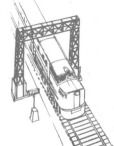

ALL ABOARD!

Probably, most of your traveling has been by car. Other kinds of travel—bus, train, or plane—are fun to find out about. The more we know, the more fun we get from life. One of the really great ways of finding out is through travel.

Each kind of travel is different. Each is better in some way than the others. Buses can often take you where no other public transportation goes. Many places in the United States don't have railroads or airports. Other than going by car, the bus is the only way to get there. A bus is the cheapest of the three kinds of transportation. Some buses are air-conditioned. Some even have washrooms.

Trains have more room for moving about than other forms of transportation. Long-distance trains usually have lounge cars and places to eat. Some even have observation cars. You can sit high in the top of them, looking at country along the way.

If overnight, you can sleep in a bed on the train. You may even have your own room, called a compartment. It is a tiny living room, bedroom, and washroom all in one.

A plane is the fastest way of traveling on long trips. The view of the earth from high in the sky is breathtaking. Mountains, rivers, and cities look like models. Flying through and above clouds gives you a feeling of being in another world.

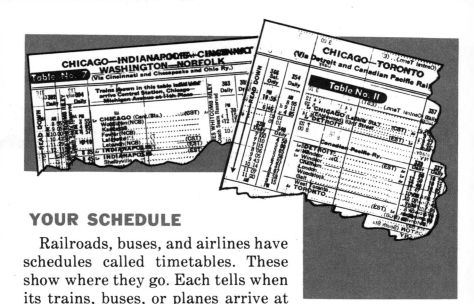

YOUR SCHEDULE

Railroads, buses, and airlines have schedules called timetables. These show where they go. Each tells when its trains, buses, or planes arrive at and leave each city.

Timetables look hard to read. They're not, really, when you learn how. There are two main things to remember. The first is the direction that the bus, train, or airplane is going. Timetables use arrows to show that. The other is that noon to midnight hours are shown in heavy type.

Read your timetable with care when you are planning a trip. Be sure that the train, bus, or plane goes on the day that you want. Railroad timetables may show that some trains don't run on Saturday.

You can get a timetable at a railroad or bus station, airline terminal or ticket office.

HOW MUCH DOES IT COST?

The third requirement asks you to figure the cost of train, bus, and plane travel. To do this, you will have to choose a city far from home. Check at the nearest stations and airports to find out the rates.

It will make a difference whether your imaginary trip is one-way or round trip. One way, the cost by bus will be about 2½ to 3 cents a mile. A train will cost from 4 to 5 cents a mile. If you are going round trip, the cost per mile will be lower.

The cost of a plane trip sometimes depends on the season. At vacation time, it may be much higher than during the rest of the year. Also, the cost can vary, even on the same plane. Going by first class or by tourist class can make the difference. Four to five cents a mile probably is the lowest cost that you can find. It may be much higher if you go first class.

Of course, you save lots of time going by plane on a very long trip. Therefore, you may save money on food and sleeping by flying. You don't have to buy meals on a plane. They are served at no extra cost.

A family taking a long trip by car can spend a lot of money. But, if you and your parents plan well, you can cut costs.

The American Automobile Association says you can figure the cost pretty closely like this:

- Car costs—gas, oil, lubrication, small repairs—will be about $35 for each 1,000 miles.
- Car storage will run about $2 per night. (If you stay in motels or at a campground, parking will probably be free.)
- A hotel or motel costs about $20 for two grown-ups. It will be a little more with your whole family.
- Meals will cost about $12 a day for an adult. It will be less for children.
- Allow about 15 percent for tips.
- If you are going to use a turnpike, add toll costs.

STOPPING OVERNIGHT

If you take a long car trip, you will need a place to sleep overnight. Some families like to drive until early evening. Then they look for a place to stay. Others set a goal for the day's driving. They make reservations by writing or calling a motel or hotel.

There are good things about both ways of doing it. If you make reservations ahead, you know you'll have a place to stay. You know, also, how much it will cost.

If you wait until evening before looking, it may be hard to find a place that has room. Then too, you may have to pay more for it than you planned. However, there is one good thing about going like this. You don't have to drive all the way if you don't want to.

Perhaps your family wants to make reservations ahead of time. You don't know the city where you'll be. What to do? Write to the Chamber of Commerce. They'll send a list of hotels and motels with rates.

Also, ask the Chamber of Commerce to send literature about the town. They'll be glad to tell you about the things to see in their area.

How far should you drive in a day? Each family must decide that for itself. Most people don't like to go too far because everybody gets tired. Besides, you don't have time for sight-seeing along the way. The distance will depend on many things. Superhighway or country road? Time for sight-seeing or steady driving? You'll also have to allow for gas, meal, and rest stops.

CAMPING TRIPS

Millions of American families take vacation trips by camping along the way. They stop when they feel like it at a public campground. They stay a day or two, then move on again. If they especially like a camp, they may stay for a week or more. This can be a cheap and very pleasant vacation. It's also good training for boys who will soon be Scouts.

There are four main kinds of public campgrounds.

NATIONAL FORESTS

There are more than 150 in the United States. National forests cover one-tenth of the whole area of our country. The U.S. Department of Agriculture controls them. They are not just for camping. Forests are used for raising trees for lumber, for raising cattle, and as protection for our watersheds. The national forests have over 2,000 campgrounds. Most have tables, benches, rock fireplaces, a water supply, and toilets. Many are free. They don't accept reservations. First come, first served.

NATIONAL PARKS

The National Park Service controls these. National parks have many natural wonders of great beauty. So, they are set aside for recreation and enjoyment for us and people of the future. Most of the national parks have campgrounds. These have a water supply, tables, fireplaces, and restrooms. Some have laundry rooms, showers, and stores. Nearly all charge a fee.

With the increase in camping interest, most campgrounds are heavily used. In the summer they are often full by noon. They don't take reservations, so planning is hard.

NATIONAL MONUMENTS

There are 80 national monuments in the United States. They are interesting to visit. Some have camping places. You might find a national monument along your route. It's worth a visit.

STATE PARKS

There are about 2,000 state parks. Some of them are for day use only, such as picnics. Some of the state parks where you can camp are highly developed. Others are very simple. Most have a small daily charge. Perhaps your family would like to know more about campsites. Check some current guidebooks on camping. Many will tell you where to write for more information about camps in each state.

Before you go on a camping vacation, try to earn your Outdoorsman badge. You'll learn many things about outdoor living that will be helpful on your trip.

ON THE ROAD

When going by train, plane, or bus, you really don't have much to do. You just pack your bag and get there on time. But when you go by car, you have to do more planning.

Your father has to be sure that the car is ready. That means making sure the brakes, lights, and steering are OK. The car must be oiled and greased. It should have plenty of gas in the tank. The tires should be checked.

You can help your father and mother get ready for the trip. First there is the planning. How do you find the best way to get where you want to go? How do you know the best roads? By using road maps.

It's easy to get maps of your own state and of neighboring ones. Go to your nearest gas station. They have free maps. They will give you what you need when you explain about your trip. If you plan well ahead, you can get free route directions too. Most oil companies offer this service. Just ask at the gas station where to write for it.

On a long trip, you'll want to decide how far to go the first day. Where will you stop? At a hotel? motel? a camping ground?

Then there's the packing to do for the trip. You should have a list to check things off. Then you'll be sure that you're not forgetting anything important.

Always have a first aid kit in the family car. It's important when the family is going on a long trip.

PACKING YOUR SUITCASE

You will want to have a suitcase with extra clothes. You may need another pair of shoes. Of course, you'll need toothbrush and toothpaste. Maybe you'll have your own suitcase. Maybe you'll share your father's.

Here are some tips on how to pack it:

- Make a list of things you'll need. Check it with mother or dad.
- Roll as many clothes as you can to save room. Press out wrinkles with your fingers as you make tight rolls. You can do this with pants, shirts, underwear, and sweaters.
- Put extra shoes at the back end of the suitcase. When the bag is standing up, they will be on the bottom. Then they won't press down and wrinkle things.
- Tuck small things like socks and handkerchiefs into the shoes to save room.
- Put your toothbrush and toothpaste in a plastic jar or bag. (A jar won't crush easily.)
- Perhaps your family's luggage all looks alike. Make it easy to tell yours. Put a name tag on your suitcase. Or mark it with colored tape. Each member of the family could use a different color. Then finding your bag should be easy.

TRAVELER
SCOREBOARD

Requirements

EARNING THE WEBELOS BADGE AND ARROW OF LIGHT AWARD

Your Webelos den leader and your den chief will help you learn the things you need to know to pass the Webelos badge and Arrow of Light award requirements. When you are ready, you will pass them to your Webelos den leader.

Your Webelos den leader and your Den Mother before him have looked forward to the day when all your hard work would result in your graduation into a Boy Scout troop.

Your parents or your guardian will be proud of you when they watch YOU stand in front of the Scoutmaster of your new troop and say the Boy Scout Oath:

> *"On my honor I will do my best*
> *To do my duty to God and my country*
> *And to obey the Scout Law;*
> *To help other people at all times;*
> *To keep myself physically strong,*
> *Mentally awake, and morally straight."*

THE WEBELOS BADGE

This is the fourth badge of rank that you may earn in the Cub Scout program. You may start to earn it as soon as you become a Webelos Scout.

As a Webelos Scout, wear it centered on the bottom of your left uniform pocket to complete the diamond of cloth badges.

THE WEBELOS BADGE
REQUIREMENTS

Approved
by

1. Earn three activity badges. .... *C. Fail*
C. Fail
C. Fail

2. Active member of the den for 3 months (attendance, dues, den projects). .... *C. Fail*

3. Show that you know and understand
the requirements to be a Boy Scout.

- Understand and intend to live by:
  The Scout Oath or Promise ....
  The Scout Law .... *C. Fail*
  The Scout slogan .... *C. Fail*

- Know the following and when to use them:
  Scout salute .... *C. Fail*
  Scout sign .... *C. Fail*
  Scout handclasp .... *C. Fail*

- Understand the significance of the Scout badge.
  Know its parts and tell what each stands for. .... _____

- Understand and agree to follow the
  Outdoor Code. .... *C. Fail*

4. Point out and explain the various parts of the
Webelos Scout uniform. Tell how a Scout uniform
is different. Tell when and when not to wear the
Scout uniform. .... *Flock*

5. Plan and lead a flag ceremony in your den. .... *Flock*

Materials to help you do these things start on page 27
in the *Boy Scout Handbook.*

THE ARROW OF LIGHT AWARD

This is the award for the highest rank in the Cub Scout program. You may start to earn it as soon as you have earned your Webelos badge.

As a Cub Scout, wear it centered on the flap of your left shirt pocket. When you become a Scout it should be centered at the bottom of the left pocket of your shirt.

The Arrow of Light award has a special meaning. Notice the Indian sign for the sun over the arrow? That's why it is called the Arrow of Light.

Notice the seven rays of the sun—one for each day of the week. They will remind you to do your best every day as you follow the arrow that leads to Scouting.

By earning and wearing the Arrow of Light award, you show Cubs and Scouts something important. They know that you are ready to be a Scout.

THE ARROW OF LIGHT REQUIREMENTS

Approved by

1. Be active in your Webelos den for at least 6 months since joining and ....   *C. Fail*

   Earned the Webelos badge ....

2. Repeat from memory the Scout Oath or Promise and the 12 points of the Scout Law. Tell how you have already practiced these in your everyday life. _____

3. Show again that you can give and explain the:

   Scout motto ....   *C. Fail*

   Scout slogan ....   *C. Fail*

   Scout sign ....   *C. Fail*

   Scout salute ....   *C. Fail*

   Scout handclasp ....   *C. Fail*

4. Show and explain how to handle the "hurry cases" in first aid ....
   (Breathing stopped, serious bleeding, and internal poisoning. Know what shock is and its relationship to the hurry cases. Know what to do for it. See First Aid Skill Award in the *Scout Handbook*. Show proper treatment for cuts and scratches and how to apply an adhesive bandage.)   *C. Fail*

5. Earn 4 more activity badges ....
   (Three were earned for Webelos badge. The total of seven must include Citizen and at least two of the following: Aquanaut, Athlete, Naturalist, or Outdoorsman.)

6. With your Webelos den, visit at least one troop meeting and ....

   One Scout-oriented outdoor activity. ....   *C. Fail*

7. Participate in a Webelos dad-and-son overnight or day hike. ....   *C. Fail*

8. After you have completed all of the above seven requirements, and after a talk with your Webelos leader, arrange to visit, with your parent or guardian, a meeting of a troop (or troops) you think you might like to join. Talk to the Scoutmaster. Then get an "Application To Become a Scout," fill it out, and have your parent sign it. Show it to your Webelos leader. ....

THE MEANING OF THE SCOUT OATH

Scouting is a game. Like all other games, it has rules you must follow to be a member of the team.

The rules of Scouting are found in the Scout Oath (or Promise), the Scout Law, the Scout motto, and the Scout slogan.

Duties are the foundation of all fair dealings. Every right in the world rests on an equal duty. For everything we get, there are things we must give. In the Scout Oath you will find a clear statement. As a Scout you have three duties: to God and your country, to other people, and to yourself.

DUTY TO GOD AND COUNTRY: Your parents and religious leaders teach you to know and love God. They show you how you can serve Him. By following these teachings, you do your duty to God. Our country was built upon a trust in God. Men and women of the past worked to make our America. They gave their lives for it when called upon. They raised it to where it is today. It is your duty to carry on. Work for your country's good. Obey its laws. Show your loyalty.

DUTY TO OTHER PEOPLE: There are many people who need help. A cheery smile and a helpful hand make life easier for others. By obeying the Scout Law and by doing a Good Turn daily, you prove yourself a Scout. You do your part to make this a happier world.

DUTY TO SELF: You owe it to yourself to take care of your body. Protect it and build it. Then you can help others. You owe it to yourself to develop your brain. Add to your knowledge. Make the best possible use of your abilities. You owe it to yourself to aim to become a man of strong character. Be ready to take your place in the world as a capable citizen.

THE SCOUT LAW

A Scout Is TRUSTWORTHY.

A Scout tells the truth. He keeps his promises. Honesty is part of his code of conduct. People can depend on him.

A Scout Is LOYAL.

A Scout is true to his family, Scout leaders, friends, school, and nation.

A Scout Is HELPFUL.

A Scout is concerned about other people. He does things willingly for others without pay or reward.

A Scout Is FRIENDLY.

A Scout is a friend to all. He is a brother to other Scouts. He seeks to understand others. He respects those with ideas and customs other than his own.

A Scout Is COURTEOUS.

A Scout is polite to everyone regardless of age or position. He knows good manners make it easier for people to get along together.

A Scout Is KIND.

A Scout understands there is strength in being gentle. He treats others as he wants to be treated. He does not hurt or kill harmless things without reason.

A Scout Is OBEDIENT.

A Scout follows the rules of his family, school, and troop. He obeys the laws of his community and country. If he thinks these rules and laws are unfair, he tries to have them changed in an orderly manner rather than disobey them.

A Scout Is CHEERFUL.

A Scout looks for the bright side of things. He cheerfully does tasks that come his way. He tries to make others happy.

A Scout Is THRIFTY.

A Scout works to pay his way and to help others. He saves for unforeseen needs. He protects and conserves natural resources. He carefully uses time and property.

A Scout Is BRAVE.

A Scout can face danger even if he is afraid. He has the courage to stand for what he thinks is right even if others laugh at or threaten him.

A Scout Is CLEAN.

A Scout keeps his body and mind fit and clean. He goes around with those who believe in living by these same ideals. He helps keep his home and community clean.

A Scout Is REVERENT.

A Scout is reverent toward God. He is faithful in his religious duties. He respects the beliefs of others.

THE SCOUT MOTTO

The Scout motto is Be Prepared. Someone once asked Baden-Powell, the founder of Scouting, "Be prepared for what?" "Why," said B-P, "for any old thing." That's just the idea. The Scout motto means that you are always in a state of readiness in mind and body to do your duty and to face danger, if necessary, to help others.

THE SCOUT SLOGAN

The Scout slogan is Do a Good Turn Daily. This does not mean that you are supposed to do one Good Turn during the day and then stop. On the contrary—it means for you to do at least one Good Turn a day. It means looking for opportunities to help and then helping, quietly and without boasting.

Remember always that a Good Turn is an extra act of kindness—not just something you do because it is good manners.

As a Scout you will learn how to do a great many things that will help you become an outdoorsman. You'll be able to take care of yourself and do GOOD TURNS that deserve capital letters. Big or small, do a Good Turn each day.

THE SCOUT SALUTE

The Scout salute signifies respect and courtesy. You use it to salute the flag of the United States of America.

To give the Scout salute, place the fingers of your right hand in position as for the Scout sign. Bring the hand smartly up to your head, palm sideways, until your forefinger touches the edge of your cap above the right eye or, if you are capless, your forehead above the right eye. When the salute is completed, snap your hand down quickly to your side.

THE SCOUT SIGN

When you have become a member, you show that you belong by using the Scout sign, salute, and handclasp and by wearing the uniform and the Scout badge.

The Scout sign identifies you as a Scout anywhere in the world. You use it when you give the Scout Oath and Law. When another boy greets you with the Scout sign, you know that he is a member of the world brotherhood of Scouting—you respond by making the Scout sign. Raise your right hand palm forward, with the three middle fingers upward and the thumb covering the nail of the little finger, upper arm straight out to the side, forearm straight up. The three upstretched fingers in the Scout sign—as well as the three fingers held together in the Scout salute—stand for the three parts of the Scout Oath; the thumb and little finger stand for the bond that ties all Scouts together.

THE SCOUT HANDCLASP

To give the Scout handclasp, you merely use your left hand instead of the right. You do not interlock your fingers.

THE SCOUT UNIFORM

WEAR THE UNIFORM: At all activities of your patrol and troop—meetings, hikes, camps, rallies. When you appear for advancement before a progress review or court of honor. When you take part in a special Scout service for your community. Throughout the Anniversary Celebration of the Boy Scouts of America in February. DO NOT WEAR THE UNIFORM: When you collect funds or take part in a selling campaign. (This does not forbid Scouts in uniform from selling tickets for Scout circuses, rallies, and similar Scouting events or selling items related to such events.) When you participate in a distinctly political activity. When you appear on the stage professionally (except by special permission).

FLAG CEREMONIES

- Have the boys give the Cub Scout salute and repeat the Pledge of Allegiance to the flag.

- Parade the American flag and the den flag past the line of Webelos Scouts who stand at attention and salute.

- Plan a ceremony on the history of the flag. Each boy in the den can make and color a different paper flag to show how our present flag was formed.

- Have the Webelos Scouts in your den march past the American flag, giving the proper salute.

276

THE SCOUT BADGE

The Scout badge was adapted from the north point of the old mariner's compass. The design is often referred to as a fleur-de-lis or the iris flower. This design, with slight changes, is used in countries around the world as a mark of the Scout brotherhood of friendliness and good citizenship.

The main part of the Scout badge signifies that a Scout is able to point the right way in life as truly as the compass points it in the field.

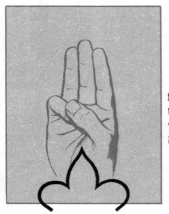

The three points, like the three fingers in the Scout sign, stand for the three parts of the Scout Oath to which a boy pledges himself as a Scout.

The stars symbolize the ideals of truth and knowledge of the Scout movement. They guide you by night and suggest a Scout's outdoor life.

truth

knowledge

The eagle with the shield is the national emblem of the United States of America. It stands for freedom and readiness to defend that freedom.

The scroll with the Scout motto is turned up at the ends to suggest the corners of a Scout's mouth raised in a smile as he does his duty.

The knot attached to the bottom of the scroll is to remind you that, as a Scout, you have promised to do a Good Turn for someone every day.

More About the
BOBCAT
REQUIREMENTS

Approved
by

1. Learn and give the Cub Scout Promise. .... _____

2. Say the Law of the Pack. Tell what it means. .... _____

3. Tell what Webelos means. .... _____

4. Show the Cub Scout sign and handshake. Tell
   what they mean. .... _____

5. Give Cub Scout motto and salute. Tell what they
   mean. .... _____

These five requirements are explained completely
on the following pages.

When you have completed them, you will be in-
ducted into the Webelos den at a special pack ceremony and be presented with your Webelos badge
colors and your Bobcat badge.

CUB SCOUT PROMISE

I, (say your name), promise
To DO MY BEST
To do my DUTY to GOD
And my COUNTRY
To HELP other people, and
To OBEY the Law of the Pack

PROMISE

When you promise to do something, you mean you will do it. Even if it is hard, a Webelos Scout keeps his promise. He wants people to believe him.

DO MY BEST

When you say "I will do my best," you mean "I will try as hard as I can." One boy's best can be better than another boy's best. Webelos den leaders do not expect you to be perfect, but they want you to do your best.

DO MY DUTY

When you do your duty, you do your share. You do what you ought to do.

Your duty to God is done with God's help. It means you practice your religion at home, in the church or synagogue, in everything you do.

Your duty to your country means being a good American. Our country's laws take care of the rights that God gives everybody in the world.

HELP

This means thinking about other people and their needs. Sometimes this is not easy. But a Webelos Scout will help others when he can.

LAW OF THE PACK

"THE WEBELOS SCOUT FOLLOWS AKELA"

Who is Akela? (Say Ah-kay'-la.)

Akela is the Webelos Scout name for a good leader. Some of the people you may call Akela are your father or mother, your teacher, your den chief, your Webelos den leader, your Cubmaster, or anybody who is a good leader.

Most good leaders first learned to follow. That's why the first part of the Law of the Pack asks you to learn to follow. Follow good leaders. Follow Akela.

"THE WEBELOS SCOUT HELPS THE PACK GO"

When you become a Webelos Scout, you are no longer just a boy. You are a member of a Webelos den and a pack. You can't think only of yourself, but you must think of your fellow Cub Scouts.

Help the pack GO by going to all meetings, by following the leaders, and by making your pack better in every way because you are in it.

"THE PACK HELPS THE WEBELOS SCOUT GROW"

You'll like the Webelos den and all of the activity badge areas. Working on the ones you like will help you learn new skills and new ways of doing things. Earning the Arrow of Light award will help you prepare for Scouting.

"THE WEBELOS SCOUT GIVES GOODWILL"

Goodwill means kindness and cheerfulness. The Webelos Scout is always looking for things to do for other people. Not big jobs but little things that help.

Smile and help—those are two fine Webelos Scout words.

"TELL WHAT WEBELOS MEANS"

WEBELOS: Say Wee'-Buh-lows.

Webelos has a secret meaning for Cub Scouts. It means: WE'll BE LOyal Scouts.

Loyal means that you will keep your Cub Scout promise.

THE HANDSHAKE

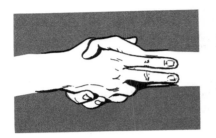

When you shake hands with another Webelos or Cub Scout, hold out your right hand just as you usually would shake hands. But put your first two fingers along the inside of the other fellow's wrist. This means that he, too, will help others and obey the Law of the Pack.

THE SIGN

Make the sign with your right hand, straight above your shoulder. This is the sign of the Cub Scout and Webelos Scout allover the world. The two top fingers stand for the two parts of the Promise— Help and Obey. Give the sign whenever you repeat the Promise or Law of the Pack.

THE MOTTO

"DO YOUR BEST." That's the Cub Scout and Webelos Scout motto. Another boy may do something better than you do it, but if you do your best you need not be ashamed.

THE SALUTE

Hold your fingers as you do for the sign, except that your first two fingers are closed together. Salute your leaders and other Webelos Scouts to show them goodwill and courtesy.

The full-size diagrams on the inside front and back covers will show you the sizes, shapes, location, and method of attaching the insignia you will be eligible to wear as a Webelos Scout.

These instructions will show your parent where to sew insignia.

SLEEVE INSIGNIA: Use the diagram on the inside back cover as a guide. (a) Center the edge of the page on the crease of the sleeve. (b) Line up shoulder seams of page and shirt. (c) Mark exact location of the badge with white chalk. (d) Pin to sleeve. Take off old insignia before putting on new.

POCKET INSIGNIA: As a Webelos Scout, you may wear the Wolf and Bear badges if you have earned them. They are worn as shown on the inside front cover. (You may wear as many Silver Arrow Points as you earn or for the sake of neatness you may choose to wear two or three on your uniform and show the rest on your trophy skin.) The Arrow of Light is centered above the button on the left pocket flap. Center temporary insignia on the right shirt pocket. The U.S. Flag emblem is worn above the Cub Scout strip over the right shirt pocket.

TO SEW: Ask your parent to locate the exact position of the insignia, and pin or baste to the shirt. Use a fine overhand, back, blind, or buttonhole stitch to sew on the insignia. Thread should match the border of the emblem.

SHOULDER CORD: Wear only when holding the office the cord stands for.